AF304313

Defoe Abbott Marx Hardy Machiavelli Montaigne Chesterton Cooper Emerson Joyce Austen Hugo Eliot Grimm
Melville Haggard
Stoker Carroll Christie Molière
Wilde Maupassant Byron Schiller
Garnett Fitzgerald Einstein Engels Smith Kafka Hall
Goethe Hawthorne Willis
Cotton Dostoyevsky
Baum Henry Kipling Doyle
Leslie Dumas Nietzsche
Flaubert Turgenev Balzac
Stockton Vatsyayana Crane
Burroughs Verne
Curtis Tocqueville Whitman Gogol Vinci
Homer Widger Tolstoy Busch
Darwin Thoreau Twain Scott Plato Harte
Potter Freud Zola Lawrence Hesse
Kant Jowett Stevenson Dickens Burton
Andersen Cervantes
London Descartes Voltaire
Poe Aristotle Wells Cooke
Hale James Hastings
Bunner Shakespeare Irving
Richter Chekhov Chambers
Doré Dante Shaw da Benedict Alcott
Swift Wodehouse Pushkin
Newton

Musical Memories

Camille Saint-Saëns

Imprint

This book is part of TREDITION CLASSICS

Author: Camille Saint-Saëns
Cover design: Buchgut, Berlin – Germany

Publisher: tredition GmbH, Hamburg - Germany
ISBN: 978-3-8424-8146-6

www.tredition.com
www.tredition.de

Copyright:
The content of this book is sourced from the public domain.

The intention of the TREDITION CLASSICS series is to make world literature in the public domain available in printed format. Literary enthusiasts and organizations, such as Project Gutenberg, worldwide have scanned and digitally edited the original texts. tredition has subsequently formatted and redesigned the content into a modern reading layout. Therefore, we cannot guarantee the exact reproduction of the original format of a particular historic edition. Please also note that no modifications have been made to the spelling, therefore it may differ from the orthography used today.

SCIRE · QVOD
SCIENDVM

Contents

Illustrations

Musical Memories

Musical Memories

Chapter I

Memories of My Childhood

In bygone days I was often told that I had two mothers, and, as a matter of fact, I did have two—the mother who gave me life and my maternal great-aunt, Charlotte Masson. The latter came from an old family of lawyers named Gayard and this relationship makes me a descendant of General Delcambre, one of the heroes of the retreat from Russia. His granddaughter married Count Durrieu of the *Académie des Inscriptions et Belles-Lettres*. My great-aunt was born in the provinces in 1781, but she was adopted by a childless aunt and uncle who made their home in Paris. He was a wealthy lawyer and they lived magnificently.

My great-aunt was a precocious child—she walked at nine months—and she became a woman of keen intellect and brilliant attainments. She remembered perfectly the customs of the *Ancien Régime*, and she enjoyed telling about them, as well as about the Revolution, the Reign of Terror, and the times that followed. Her family was ruined by the Revolution and the slight, frail, young girl undertook to earn her living by giving lessons in French, on the pianoforte—the instrument was a novelty then—in singing, painting, embroidery, in fact in everything she knew and in much that she did not. If she did not know, she learned then and there so that she could teach. Afterwards, she married one of her cousins. As she had no children of her own, she brought one of her nieces from Champagne and adopted her. This niece was my mother, Clemence Collin. The Massons were about to retire from business with a comfortable fortune, when they lost practically everything within two weeks, in a panic, saving just enough to live decently. Shortly after this my mother married my father, a minor official in the Department of the Interior. My great-uncle died of a broken heart some months before my birth on October 9, 1835. My father died of consumption on the thirty-first of the following December, just a year to a day after his marriage.

Thus the two women were both left widows, poorly provided for, weighed down by sad memories, and with the care of a delicate child. In fact I was so delicate that the doctors held out little hope of my living, and on their advice I was left in the country with my nurse until I was two years old.

While my aunt had had a remarkable education, my mother had not been so widely taught. But she made up for any lack by the display of an imagination and an eager power of assimilation which bordered on the miraculous. She often told me about an uncle who was very fond of her—he had been ruined in the cause of Philippe Egalité. This uncle was an artist, but he was, nevertheless, passionately fond of music. He had even built with his own hands a concert organ on which he used to play. My mother used to sit between his knees and, while he amused himself by running his fingers through her splendid black hair, he would talk to her about art, music, painting—beauty in every form. So she got it into her head that if she ever had sons of her own, the first should be a musician, the second a painter, and the third a sculptor. As a result, when I came home from the nurse, she was not greatly surprised that I began to listen to every noise and to every sound; that I made the doors creak, and would plant myself in front of the clocks to hear them strike. My special delight was the music of the tea-kettle—a large one which was hung before the fire in the drawing-room every morning. Seated nearby on a small stool, I used to wait with a lively curiosity for the first murmurs of its gentle and variegated *crescendo*, and the appearance of a microscopic oboe which gradually increased its song until it was silenced by the kettle boiling. Berlioz must have heard that oboe as well as I, for I rediscovered it in the "Ride to Hell" in his *La Damnation de Faust*.

At the same time I was learning to read. When I was two-years-and-a-half old, they placed me in front of a small piano which had not been opened for several years. Instead of drumming at random as most children of that age would have done, I struck the notes one after another, going on only when the sound of the previous note had died away. My great-aunt taught me the names of the notes and got a tuner to put the piano in order. While the tuning was going on, I was playing in the next room, and they were utterly astonished when I named the notes as they were sounded. I was not told all these details—I remember them perfectly.

I was taught by Le Carpentier's method and I finished it in a month. They couldn't let a little monkey like that work away at the piano, and I cried like a lost soul when they closed the instrument. Then they left it open and put a small stool in front of it. From time to time I would leave my playthings and climb up to drum out whatever came into my head. Gradually, my great-aunt, who fortunately had an excellent foundation in music, taught me how to hold my hands properly so that I did not acquire the gross faults which are so difficult to correct later on. But they did not know what sort of music to give me. That written especially for children is, as a rule, entirely melody and the part for the left hand is uninteresting. I refused to learn it. "The bass doesn't sing," I said, in disgust.

Then they searched the old masters, in Haydn and Mozart, for things sufficiently easy for me to handle. At five I was playing small sonatas correctly, with good interpretation and excellent precision. But I consented to play them only before listeners capable of appreciating them. I have read in a biographical sketch that I was threatened with whippings to make me play. That is absolutely false; but it was necessary to tell me that there was a lady in the audience who was an excellent musician and had fastidious tastes. I would not play for those who did not know.

As for the threat of whippings, that must be relegated to the realm of legends with the one that Garcia punished his daughters to make them learn to sing. Madame Viardot expressly told me that neither she nor her sister was abused by their father and that they learned music without realizing it, just as they learned to talk.

But in spite of my surprising progress my teacher did not foresee what my future was to be. "When he is fifteen," she said, "if he can write a dance, I shall be satisfied." It was just at this time, however, that I began to write music. I wrote waltzes and galops—the galop was fashionable at that period; it ran to rather ordinary musical motives and mine were no exception to the rule. Liszt had to show by his *Galop Chromatique* the distinction that genius can give to the most commonplace themes. My waltzes were better. As has always been the case with me, I was already composing the music directly on paper without working it out on the piano. The waltzes were too difficult for my hands, so a friend of the family, a sister of the singer Geraldy, was kind enough to play them for me.

I have looked over these little compositions lately. They are insignificant, but it is impossible to find a technical error in them. Such precision was remarkable for a child who had no idea of the science of harmony. About that time some one had the notion that I should hear an orchestra. So they took me to a symphony concert and my mother held me in her arms near the door. Until then I had only heard single violins and their tone had not pleased me. But the impression of the orchestra was entirely different and I listened with delight to a passage played by a quartet, when, suddenly, came a blast from the brass instruments—the trumpets, trombones and cymbals. I broke into loud cries, "Make them stop. They prevent my hearing the music." They had to take me out.

When I was seven, I passed out of my great-aunt's hands into Stamaty's. He was surprised at the way my education in music had been directed and he expressed this in a small work in which he discussed the necessity of making a correct start. In my case, he said, there was nothing to do but to perfect.

Stamaty was Kalkbrenner's best pupil and the propagator of the method he had invented. This method was based on the *guide main*, so I was put to work on it. The preface to Kalkbrenner's method, in which he relates the beginnings of his invention, is exceedingly interesting. This invention consisted of a rod placed in front of the keyboard. The forearm rested on this rod in such a way that all muscular action save that of the hand was suppressed. This system is excellent for teaching the young pianist how to play pieces written for the harpsichord or the first pianofortes where the keys responded to slight pressure; but it is inadequate for modern works and instruments. It is the way one ought to begin, for it develops firmness of the fingers and suppleness of the wrist, and, by easy stages, adds the weight of the forearm and of the whole arm. But in our day it has become the practice to begin at the end. We learn the elements of the fugue from Sebastian Bach's *Wohltemperirte Klavier*, the piano from the works of Schumann and Liszt, and harmony and instrumentation from Richard Wagner. All too often we waste our efforts, just as singers who learn rôles and rush on the stage before they know how to sing ruin their voices in a short time.

Firmness of the fingers is not the only thing that one learns from Kalkbrenner's method, for there is also a refinement of the quality of the sound made by the fingers alone, a valuable resource which is unusual in our day.

Unfortunately, this school invented as well continuous *legato*, which is both false and monotonous; the abuse of nuances, and a mania for continual *expressio* used with no discrimination. All this was opposed to my natural feelings, and I was unable to conform to it. They reproached me by saying that I would never get a really fine effect—to which I was entirely indifferent.

When I was ten, my teacher decided that I was sufficiently prepared to give a concert in the Salle Pleyel, so I played there, accompanied by an Italian orchestra, with Tilmant as the conductor. I gave Beethoven's *Concerto in C minor* and one of Mozart's concertos in B flat. There was some question of my playing at the Société des Concerts du Conservatoire, and there was even a rehearsal. But Seghers, who afterwards founded the Société St. Cécile, was a power in the affairs of the orchestra. He detested Stamaty and told him that the Société was not organized to play children's accompaniments. My mother felt hurt and wanted to hear nothing more of it.

After my first concert, which was a brilliant success, my teacher wanted me to give others, but my mother did not wish me to have a career as an infant prodigy. She had higher ambitions and was unwilling for me to continue in concert work for fear of injuring my health. The result was that a coolness sprang up between my teacher and me which ended our relations.

At that time my mother made a remark which was worthy of Cornelia. One day some one remonstrated with her for letting me play Beethoven's sonatas. "What music will he play when he is twenty?" she was asked. "He will play his own," was her reply.

The greatest benefit I got from my experience with Stamaty was my acquaintance with Maleden, whom he gave me as my teacher in composition. Maleden was born in Limoges, as his accent always showed. He was thin and long-haired, a kind and timid soul, but an incomparable teacher. He had gone to Germany in his youth to study with a certain Gottfried Weber, the inventor of a system which Maleden brought back with him and perfected. He made it a wonderful tool with which to get to the depths of music—a light for the darkest corners. In this system the chords are not considered in and for themselves—as fifths, sixths, sevenths—but in relation to the pitch of the scale on which they appear. The chords acquire different characteristics according to the place they occupy, and, as a result, certain things are explained which are, otherwise, inexplicable. This method is taught in the Ecole Niedermeuer, but I don't know that it is taught elsewhere.

Maleden was extremely anxious to become a professor at the Conservatoire. As the result of powerful influence, Auber was about to sign Maleden's appointment, when, in his scrupulous honesty, he thought he ought to write and warn him that his method differed entirely from that taught in the institution. Auber was frightened and Maleden was not admitted.

Our lessons were often very stormy. From time to time certain questions came up on which I could not agree with him. He would then take me quietly by the ear, bend my head and hold my ear to the table for a minute or two. Then, he would ask whether I had changed my mind. As I had not, he would think it over and very often he would confess that I was right.

"Your childhood," Gounod once told me, "wasn't musical." He was wrong, for he did not know the many tokens of my childhood. Many of my attempts are unfinished—to say nothing of those I destroyed—but among them are songs, choruses, cantatas, and overtures, none of which will ever see the light. Oblivion will enshroud these gropings after effect, for they are of no interest to the public. Among these scribblings I have found some notes written in pencil when I was four. The date on them leaves no doubt about the time of their production.

Chapter II

The Old Conservatoire

I cannot let the old Conservatoire in the Rue Bergère go without paying it a last farewell, for I loved it deeply as we all love the things of our youth. I loved its antiquity, the utter absence of any modern note, and its atmosphere of other days. I loved that absurd court with the wailing notes of sopranos and tenors, the rattling of pianos, the blasts of trumpets and trombones, the arpeggios of clarinets, all uniting to form that ultra-polyphone which some of our composers have tried to attain—but without success. Above all I loved the memories of my education in music which I obtained in that ridiculous and venerable palace, long since too small for the pupils who thronged there from all parts of the world.

I was fourteen when Stamaty, my piano teacher, introduced me to Benoist, the teacher of the organ, an excellent and charming man, familiarly known as "Father Benoist." They put me in front of the keyboard, but I was badly frightened, and the sounds I made were so extraordinary that all the pupils shouted with laughter. I was received at the Conservatoire as an "auditor."

So there I was only admitted to the honor of listening to others. I was extremely painstaking, however, and I never lost a note or one of the teacher's words. I worked and thought at home, studying hard on Sebastian Bach's *Wohltemperirte Klavier*. All of the pupils, however, were not so industrious. One day, when they had all failed and Benoist, as a result, had nothing to do, he put me at the organ. This time no one laughed and I at once became a regular pupil. At the end of the year I won the second prize. I would have had the first except for my youth and the inconvenience of having me leave a class where I needed to stay longer.

That same year Madeleine Brohan won the first prize in comedy. She competed with a selection from *Misanthrope*, and Mlle. Jouassin gave the other part of the dialogue. Mlle. Jouassin's technique was the better, but Madeleine Brohan was so wonderful in beauty and voice that she carried off the prize. The award made a great uproar. To-day, in such a case, the prize would be divided. Mlle. Jouassin won her prize the following year. After leaving school, she accepted and held for a long time an important place at the Comédie-Française.

Benoist was a very ordinary organist, but an admirable teacher. A veritable galaxy of talent came from his class. He had little to say, but as his taste was refined and his judgment sure, nothing he said lacked weight or authority. He collaborated in several ballets for the Opéra and that gave him a good deal of work to do. It sounds incredible, but he used to bring his "work" to class and scribble away on his orchestration while his pupils played the organ. This did not prevent his listening and looking after them. He would leave his work and make appropriate comments as though he had no other thought.

In addition to his ballets, Benoist did other little odd jobs for the Opéra. As a result one day, without thinking, he gave me the key to a deep secret. In his famous *Traité d'Instrumentation* Berlioz spoke of his admiration for a passage in Sacchini's *Œdipus à Colone*. Two clarinets are heard in descending thirds of real charm just before the words, "*Je connus la charmante Eriphyle.*" Berlioz was enthusiastic and wrote:

"We might believe that we really see Eriphyle chastely kiss his eyes. It is admirable. And yet," he adds, "there is no trace of this effect in Sacchini's score."

Now Sacchini, for some reason or other which I do not know, did not use clarinets once in the whole score. Benoist was commissioned to add them when the work was revived, as he told me as we were chatting one day. Berlioz did not know this, and Benoist, who had not read Berlioz's *Traité*, knew nothing of the romantic musician's enthusiastic admiration of his work. These happily turned thirds, although they weren't Sacchini's, were, none the less, an excellent innovation.

Benoist was less happy when he was asked to put some life into Bellini's *Romeo* by using earsplitting outbursts of drums, cymbals, and brass. During the same noise-loving period Costa, in London, gave Mozart's *Don Juan* the same treatment. He let loose throughout the opera the trombones which the author intentionally reserved for the end. Benoist ought to have refused to do such a barbarous piece of work. However, it had no effect in preventing the failure of a worthless piece, staged at great expense by the management which had rejected Les Troyens.

I was fifteen when I entered Halévy's class. I had already completed the study of harmony, counterpoint and fugue under Maleden's direction. As I have said, his method was that taught at the Ecole Niedermeuer. Faure, Messager, Perilhou, and Gigot were trained there and they taught this method in turn. My class-work consisted in making attempts at vocal and instrumental music and orchestration. My *Rêverie*, *La Feuille de Peuplier* and many other things first appeared there. They have been entirely forgotten, and rightly, for my work was very uneven.

At the end of his career Halévy was constantly writing opera and opéra-comique which added nothing to his fame and which disappeared never to be revived after a respectable number of performances. He was entirely absorbed in his work and, as a result, he neglected his classes a good deal. He came only when he had time. The pupils, however, came just the same and gave each other instruction which was far less indulgent than the master's, for his greatest fault was an overweening good nature. Even when he was at class he couldn't protect himself from self-seekers. Singers of all sorts, male and female, came for a hearing. One day it was Marie Cabel, still youthful and dazzling both in voice and beauty. Other days impossible tenors wasted his time. When the master sent word that he wasn't coming—this happened often—I used to go to the library, and there, as a matter of fact, I completed my education. The amount of music, ancient and modern, I devoured is beyond belief.

But it wasn't enough just to read music—I needed to hear it. Of course there was the Société des Concerts, but it was a Paradise, guarded by an angel with a flaming sword, in the form of a porter named Lescot. It was his duty to prevent the profane defiling the sanctuary. Lescot was fond of me and appreciated my keen desire to hear the orchestra. As a result he made his rounds as slowly as possible in order to put me out only as a last resort. Fortunately for me, Marcelin de Fresne gave me a place in his box, which I was permitted to occupy for several years.

I used to read and study the symphonies before I heard them and I saw grave defects in the Société's vaunted execution. No one would stand them now, but then they passed unnoticed. I was naïve and lacked discretion, and so I often pointed out these defects. It can be easily imagined what vials of wrath were poured on me.

As far as the public was concerned, the great success of these concerts was due to the incomparable charm of the depth of tone, which was attributed to the hall. The members of the Société believed this, too, and they would let no other orchestra be heard there. This state of affairs lasted until Anton Rubinstein got permission from the Minister of Fine Arts to give a concert there, accompanied by the Colonne orchestra. The Société fretted and fumed at this and threatened to give up its series of concerts. But the Société was overruled and the concert was given. To the general surprise it was seen that another orchestra in the same hall produced an entirely different effect. The depth of tone which had been appreciated so highly, it was found, was due to the famous Société itself, to the character of the instruments and the execution.

Nevertheless, the hall is excellent, although it is no longer adequate for the presentation of modern compositions. But it is a marvellous place for the numerous concerts given by virtuosi, both singers and instrumentalists, accompanied by an orchestra, and for chamber music. Finally, the hall where France was introduced to the masterpieces of Haydn, Mozart and Beethoven, whose influence has been so profound, is a historic place.

Numerous improvements in the administration of the Conservatoire have been introduced during the last few years. On the other hand, old and honored customs have disappeared and we can but regret their loss. From Auber's time on there was a *pension* connected with the Conservatoire. Here the young singers who came from the provinces at eighteen found board and lodging, a regular life, and a protection from the temptations of a large city, so dangerous to fresh young voices. Bouhy, Lassalle, Capoul, Gailhard and many others who have made the French stage famous came from this *pension*.

We also used to have dramatic recitals which were excellent both for the performers and the audiences as they gave works which were not in the usual repertoire. In these recitals they gave Méhul's *Joseph*, which had disappeared from the stage for a long time. The beautiful choruses sung by the fresh voices of the pupils made such a success and the whole work was so enthusiastically applauded that it was revived at the Opéra-Comique and won back a success which it has never lost. We also heard there Gluck's *Orphée* long before that masterpiece was revived at the Théâtre-Lyrique. Then there was Méhul's *Irato*, a curious and charming work which the Opéra took up afterwards. And there, too, they gave the last act of Rossini's *Otello*. The tempest in that act gave me the idea of the one which rumbles through the second act of *Samson*.

When the hall was reconstructed, the stage was destroyed so that such performances are impossible. But to make up for this, they installed a concert organ, a necessary adjunct for musical performances.

Finally, in Auber's day and even in that of Ambroise Thomas, the director was master. No one had dreamed of creating a committee, which, under cover of the director's responsibility, would strangely diminish his authority. The only benefit from the new system has been the end of the incessant war which the musical critics waged on the director. But that did no harm, either to the director or to the school, for the latter kept on growing to such an extent that it ought to have been enlarged long ago. The committee plan has won and the incident is closed. One may only hope that steps will be taken to make possible an increase in the number of pupils since so many candidates apply each year and so few are chosen.

As everyone knows, we have been struck by a perfect mania for reforms, so there is no harm in proposing one for the Conservatoire. Foreign conservatoires have been studied and they want to introduce some of their features here. As a matter of fact, some of the foreign conservatoires are housed in magnificent palaces and their curricula are elaborated with a care worthy of admiration. Whether they turn out better pupils than we do is an open question. It is beyond dispute, however, that many young foreigners come to us for their education.

Some of the reformers are scandalized at the sight of a musician in charge of a school where elocution is taught. They forget that a musician may also be a man of letters—the present director combines these qualifications—and that it is improbable that it will be different in the future. The teachers of elocution have always been the best that could be found. Although M. Faure is a musician, he has known how to bring back the classes in tragedy to their original purpose. For a time they tended towards an objectionable modernism, for they substituted in their competitions modern prose for the classic verse. And the study of the latter is very profitable.

Not only is there no harm in this union of elocution and music, but it would be useful if singers and composers would take advantage of it to familiarize themselves with the principles of diction, which, in my opinion, are indispensable to both. Instead, they distrust melody. Declamation is no longer wanted in operas, and the singers make the works incomprehensible by not articulating the words. The composers tend along the same lines, for they give no indication or direction of how they want the words spoken. All this is regrettable and should be reformed.

As you see, I object to the mania for reform and end by suggesting reforms myself. Well, one must be of one's own time, and there is no escaping the contagion.

Chapter III

Victor Hugo

Everything in my youth seemed calculated to keep me far removed from romanticism. Those about me talked only of the great classics and I saw them welcome Ponsard's *Lucrece* as a sort of Minerva whose lance was to route Victor Hugo and his foul crew, of whom they never spoke save with detestation.

Who was it, I wonder, who had the happy idea of giving me, elegantly bound, the first volumes of Victor Hugo's poems? I have forgotten who it was, but I remember what joy the vibrations of his lyre gave me. Until that time poetry had seemed to me something cold, respectable and far-away, and it was much later that the living beauty of our classics was revealed to me. I found myself at once stirred to the depths, and, as my temperament is essentially musical in everything, I began to sing them.

People have told me *ad nauseam* (and they still tell me so) that beautiful verse is inimical to music, or rather that music is inimical to good verse; that music demands ordinary verse, rhymed prose, rather than verse, which is malleable and reducible as the composer wishes. This generalization is assuredly true, if the music is written first and then adapted to the words, but that is not the ideal harmony between two arts which are made to supplement each other. Do not the rhythmic and sonorous passages of verse naturally call for song to set them off, since singing is but a better method of declaiming them? I made some attempts at this and some of those which have been preserved are: *Puisque ici bas toute âme, Le Pas d'armes du roi Jean*, and *La Cloche*. They were ridiculed at the time, but destined to some success later. Afterwards I continued with *Si tu veux faisons un réve*, which Madame Carvalho sang a good deal, *Soirée en mer*, and many others.

The older I grew the greater became my devotion to Hugo. I waited impatiently for each new work of the poet and I devoured it as soon as it appeared. If I heard about me the spiteful criticisms of irritating critics, I was consoled by talking to Berlioz who honored me with his friendship and whose admiration for Hugo equalled mine. In the meantime my literary education was improving, and I made the acquaintance of the classics and found immortal beauties in them. My admiration for the classics, however, did not diminish my regard for Hugo, for I never could see why it was unfaithfulness to him not to despise Racine. It was fortunate for me that this was my view, for I have seen the most fiery romanticists, like Meurice and Vacquerie, revert to Racine in their later years, and repair the links in a golden chain which should never have been broken.

The Empire fell and Victor Hugo came back to Paris. So I was going to have a chance of realizing my dream of seeing him and hearing his voice! But I dreaded meeting him almost as much as I wished to do so. Like Rossini Victor Hugo received his friends every evening. He came forward with both hands outstretched and told me what pleasure it was for him to see me at his house. Everything whirled around me!

"I cannot say the same to you," I answered. "I wish I were somewhere else." He laughed heartily and showed that he knew how to overcome my bashfulness. I waited to hear some of the conversation which, according to my preconceived ideas, would be in the style of his latest romance. However, it was entirely different; simple polished phrases, entirely logical, came from that "mouth of mystery."

I went to Hugo's evenings as often as possible, for I never could drink my fill of the presence of the hero of my youthful dreams. I had occasion to note to what an extent a fiery republican, a modern Juvenal, whose verses branded "kings" as if with a red hot iron, in his private life was susceptible to their flattery. The Emperor of Brazil had called on him, and the next day he could not stop talking about it constantly. Rather ostentatiously he called him "Don Pedro d'Alcantara." In French this would be "M. Pierre du Pont." Spanish inherently gives such florid sounds to ordinary names. This florid style is not frequent in French, and that is precisely what Corneille and Victor Hugo succeeded in giving it.

A slight incident unfortunately changed my relations with the great poet.

"As long as Mlle. Bertin was alive," he told me, "I would never permit *La Esmeralda* to be set to music; but if some musician should now ask for this poem, I would be glad to let him have it."

The invitation was obvious. Yet, as is generally known, this dramatic and lyric adaptation of the famous romance is not particularly happy. I was much embarrassed and I pretended not to understand, but I never dared to go to Hugo's house again.

Years passed. In 1881 a subscription was taken up to erect a statue to the author of *La Légende des Siècles*, and they began to plan celebrations for its dedication, particularly a big affair at the Trocadéro. My imagination took fire at the idea, and I wrote my *Hymne à Victor Hugo*.

As is well known, the master knew nothing at all about music, and the same was true of those around him. It is a matter of conjecture how the master and his followers happened to mistake some absurd and formless motif for one of Beethoven's sublime inspirations. Victor Hugo adapted the beautiful verses of *Stella* to this halting motif. It was published as an appendix in the *Châtiments*, with a remark about the union of two geniuses, the fusion of the verse of a great poet with the *admirable* verse of a great musician. And the poet would have Mme. Drouet play this marvellous music on the piano from time to time! *Tristia Herculis!*

As I wanted to put in my hymn something peculiar to Victor Hugo, which could not possibly be attributed to anyone else, I tried to introduce this motif of which he was so fond. And, by means of numerous tricks which every musician has up his sleeve, I managed to give it the form and character which it had lacked.

The subscription did not go fast enough to suit the master, and he had it stopped. So I put my hymn in a drawer and waited for a better opportunity.

About this time M. Bruneau, the father of the well-known composer, conceived the idea of giving spring concerts at the Trocadéro. Bruneau came to see me and asked me if I had some unpublished work which I would let him have. This was an excellent occasion for the presentation of my *Hymne*, as it had been written with the Trocadéro in mind. The performance was decided on and Victor Hugo was invited to come and hear it.

The performance was splendid—a large orchestra, the magnificent organ, eight harps, and eight trumpets sounding their flourishes in the organ loft, and a large chorus for the peroration of such splendor that it was compared to the set pieces at the close of a display of fireworks. The reception and ovation which the crowd gave the great poet, who rarely appeared in public, was beyond description. The honeyed incense of the organ, harps and trumpets was new to him and pleased his Olympian nostrils.

"Dine with me to-night," he said to me. And from that day on, I often dined with him informally with M. and Mme. Lockrou, Meurice, Vacquerie and other close friends. The fare was delightful and unpretentious, and the conversation was the same. The master sat at the head of the table, with his grandson and granddaughter on either side, saying little but always something apropos. Thanks to his vigor, his strong sonorous voice, and his quiet good humor, he did not seem like an old man, but rather like an ageless and immortal being, whom Time would never touch. His presence was just Jove-like enough to inspire respect without chilling his followers. These small gatherings, which I fully appreciated, are among the most precious recollections of my life.

Time, alas, goes on, and that fine intellect, which had ever been unclouded, began to give signs of aberration. One day he said to an Italian delegation, "The French are Italians; the Italians are French. French and Italians ought to go to Africa together and found the United States of Europe."

The red rays of twilight announced the oncoming night.

Those who saw them will never forget his grandiose funeral ceremonies, that casket under the Arc de Triomphe, covered with a veil of crape, and that immense crowd which paid homage to the greatest lyric poet of the century.

There was a committee to make musical preparations and I was a member. The most extraordinary ideas were proposed. One man wanted to have the *Marseillaise* in a minor key. Another wanted violins, for "violins produce an excellent effect in the open air." Naturally we got nowhere.

The great procession started in perfect order, but, as in all long processions, gaps occurred. I was astonished to find myself in the middle of the Champs Elysées, in a wide open space, with no one near me but Ferdinand de Lesseps, Paul Bert, and a member of the Académie, whose name I shall not mention as he is worthy of all possible respect.

De Lesseps was then at the height of his glory, and from time to time applause greeted him as he passed.

Suddenly the Academician leaned over and whispered in my ear,

"Evidently they are applauding us."

Chapter IV

The History of an Opéra-Comique

Young musicians often complain, and not without reason, of the difficulties of their careers. It may, perhaps, be useful to remind them that their elders have not always had beds of roses, and that too often they have had to breast both wind and sea after spending their best years in port, unable to make a start. These obstacles frequently are the result of the worst sort of malignity, when it is for the best interest of everyone—both of the theatres which rebuff them, and the public which ignores them—that they be permitted to set out under full sail.

In 1864 one of the most brilliant of the reviews had the following comments to make on this subject:

> Our real duty—and it is a true kindness—is not to encourage them (beginners) but to discourage them. In art a vocation is everything, and a vocation needs no one, for God aids. What use is it to encourage them and their efforts when the public obstinately refuses to pay any attention to them? If an act is ordered from one of them, it fails to go. Two or three years later the same thing is tried again with the same result. No theatre, even if it were four times as heavily subsidized as the Théâtre-Lyrique, could continue to exist on such resources. So the result is that they turn to accredited talent and call on such men from outside as Gounod, Felicien David and Victor Massé. The younger composers at once shout treason and scandal. Then, they select masterpieces by Mozart and Weber and there are the same outcries and recriminations. In the final analysis where are these young composers of genius? Who are they and what are their names? Let them go to the orchestra and hear *Le Nozze di Figaro*, *Obéron*, *Freischutz* and *Orphée* ... we are doing something for them by placing such models before them.

The young composers who were thus politely invited to be seated included, among others, Bizet, Delibes, Massenet, and the writer of these lines. Massenet and I would have been satisfied with writing a ballet for the Opéra. He proposed the *Rat Catcher* from an old German tale, while I proposed *Une nuit de Cléopâtra* on the text of Théophile Gautier. They refused us the honor, and, when they consented to order a ballet from Delibes, they did not dare to trust him with the whole work. They let him do only one act and the other was given to a Hungarian composer. As the experiment succeeded, they allowed Delibes to write, without assistance, his marvellous *Coppélia*. But Delibes had the legitimate ambition of writing a grand opera. He never reached so far.

The Paris Opéra

Bizet and I were great friends and we told each other all our troubles. "You're less unfortunate than I am," he used to tell me. "You can do something besides things for the stage. I can't. That's my only resource."

When Bizet put on the delightful *Pêcheurs de Perles*—he was helped by powerful influences—there was a general outcry and an outbreak of abuse. The Devil himself straight from Hell would not have received a worse reception. Later on, as we know, *Carmen* was received in the same way.

I was, indeed, able to do something beside work for the stage, and it was just that which closed the stage to me. I was a writer of symphonies, an organist and a pianist, so how could I be capable of writing an opera! The qualities which go to make a pianist were in a particularly bad light in the greenroom. Bizet played the piano admirably, but he never dared to play in public for fear of making his position worse.

I suggested to Carvalho that I write a *Macbeth* for Madame Viardot. Naturally enough he preferred to put on Verdi's *Macbeth*. It was an utter failure and cost him thirty thousand francs.

They tried to interest a certain princess, a patron of the arts, in my behalf. "What," she replied, "isn't he satisfied with his position? He plays the organ at the Madeleine and the piano at my house. Isn't that enough for him?"

But that wasn't enough for me, and to overcome the obstacles, I caused a scandal. At the age of twenty-eight I competed for the *Prix de Rome*! They did not give it to me on the ground that I didn't need it, but the day after the award, Auber, who was very fond of me, asked Carvalho for a libretto for me. Carvalho gave me *Le Timbre d'Argent*, which he didn't know what to do with as several musicians had refused to touch it. There were good reasons for this, for, despite an excellent foundation for the music, the libretto had serious faults. I demanded that Barbier and Carré, the authors, should make important changes, which they did at once. Then, I retired to the heights of Louveciennes and in two months wrote the score of the five acts which the work had at first.

I had to wait two years before Carvalho would consent to hear the music. Finally, worn out by my importunities, they decided to get rid of me, so Carvalho invited me to dine with him and to bring my score. After dinner I went to the piano. Carvalho was on one side and Madame Carvalho on the other. Both were very pleasant and charming, but the real meaning of this friendliness did not escape me.

They had no doubts about what awaited them. Both really loved music and little by little they fell under the spell. Serious attention succeeded the false friendliness. At the end they were enthusiastic. Carvalho declared that he would have the study of the work begun as soon as possible; it was a masterpiece; it would have a great success, but to assure this success, Madame Carvalho must sing the principal part.

Now the principal part in *Le Timbre d'Argent* is that of a dancer and the singer's part is greatly subordinate. To remedy this they decided to develop the part. Barbier invented a pretty situation to bring in the passage *Bonheur est chose legère*, but that wasn't enough. Barbier and Carré racked their brains without finding any solution of the difficulty, for on the stage as elsewhere there are problems that can't be solved.

Between times they tried to find a dancer of the first rank. Finally, they found one who had recently left the Opéra, although still at the height of her beauty and talent. And they continued to seek a way to make the part of Hélène worthy of Madame Carvalho.

The famous director had one mania. He wanted to collaborate in every work he staged. Even a work hallowed by time and success had to bear his mark; much greater were his reasons for interpolating in a new work. He would announce brusquely that the period or the country in which the action of the work took place must be changed. He tormented us for a long time to make the dancer into a singer on his wife's account. Later, he wanted to introduce a second dancer. With the exception of the prologue and epilogue the action of the piece takes place in a dream, and he took upon himself the invention of the most bizarre combinations. He even proposed to me one day to introduce wild animals. Another time he wanted to cut out all the music with the exception of the choruses and the dancer's part, and have the rest played by a dramatic company. Later, as they were rehearsing Hamlet at the Opéra and it was rumored that Mlle. Nilsson was going to play a water scene, he wanted Madame Carvalho to go to the bottom of a pool to find the fatal bell.

Foolishness of this kind took up two years.

Finally, we gave up the idea of Mme. Carvalho's coöperation. The part of Hélène was given to beautiful Mlle. Schroeder and the rehearsals began. They were interrupted by the failure of the Théâtre-Lyrique.

Shortly afterwards Perrin asked for *Le Timbre d'Argent* for the Opéra. The adaptation of the work for the large stage at the Opéra necessitated important modifications. The whole of the dialogue had to be set to music and the authors went to work on it. Perrin gave us Madame Carvalho for Hélène and Faure for Spiridion, but he wanted to burlesque the part for the tenor and give it to Mlle. Wertheimber. He wanted to engage her and had no other part for her. This was impossible. After several discussions Perrin yielded to the obstinate refusals of the authors, but I saw clearly from his attitude that he would never play our work.

About that time du Locle took over the management of the Opéra-Comique. He saw that Perrin, who was his uncle, had decided not to stage *Le Timbre d'Argent* and asked me for it.

This meant another metamorphosis for the work and new and considerable work for the musician. And this work was by no means easy. Until this time Barbier and Carré had been as close friends as Orestes and Pylades, but now they had a falling out. What one proposed, the other systematically refused. One lived in Paris; the other in the country. I went from Paris to the country and from the country to Paris trying to get these warring brothers to agree. This going to and fro lasted all summer, and then the temporary enemies came to an understanding and became as friendly as ever.

We seemed to be nearly at the end of our troubles. Du Locle had found a wonderful dancer in Italy on whom we depended, but the dancer turned out not to be one at all. She was a *mime*, and did not dance.

As there was no time to look for another dancer that season du Locle, to keep me patient, had me write with Louis Gallet *La Princesse Jaune*, with which I made my debut on the stage. I was thirty-five! This harmless little work was received with the fiercest hostility. "It is impossible to tell," wrote Jouvin, a much feared critic of the time, "in what key or in what time the overture is written." And to show me how utterly wrong I was, he told me that the public was "a compound of angles and shadows." His prose was certainly more obscure than my music.

Finally, a real dancer was engaged in Italy. It seemed as though nothing more could prevent the appearance of the unfortunate *Timbre*. "I can't believe it," I said. "Some catastrophe will put us off again."

War came!

When that frightful crisis was at an end, the dancer was re-engaged. The parts were read to the artists, and the next day Amédé Achard threw up his rôle, declaring that it belonged to grand opera and was beyond the powers of an opéra-comique tenor. It is well known that he ended his career at the Opéra.

Another tenor had to be found, but tenors are rare birds and we were unable to get one. To use the dancer he had engaged du Locle had Gallet and Guiraud improvise a short act, *Le Kobold*, which met with great success. The dancer was exquisite. Then du Locle lost interest in *Le Timbre d'Argent* and then came the failure of the Opéra-Comique.

During all these tribulations I was preparing *Samson*, although I could find no one who even wanted to hear me speak of it. They all thought that I must be mad to attempt a Biblical subject. I gave a hearing of the second act at my house, but no one understood it at all. Without the aid of Liszt, who did not know a note of it, but who engaged me to finish it and put it on at Weimar, *Samson* would never have seen the light. Afterwards it was refused in succession by Halanzier, Vaucorbeil, and Ritt and Gailhard, who decided to take it only after they had heard it sung by that admirable singer Rosine Bloch.

But to return to *Le Timbre d'Argent*. I was again on the street with my score under my arm. About that time Vizentini revived the Théâtre-Lyrique. His first play was *Paul et Virginie*, a wonderful success, and he was preparing for the close of the season another work which he liked. They were kindly disposed to me at the Ministry of Fine Arts and they interested themselves in my misfortunes. So they gave the Théâtre-Lyrique a small subsidy on condition that they play my work. I came to the theatre as one who has meddled and I quickly recognized the discomforts of my position. First, there was a search for a singer; then, for a tenor, and they tried several without success. I found a tenor who, according to all reports, was of the first rank, but, after several days of negotiation, the matter was dropped. I learned later from the artist that the manager intended to engage him for only four performances, evidently planning that the work should be played only four times.

The choice finally fell on Blum. He had a fine voice, and was a perfect singer but no actor. Indeed he said he didn't want to be an actor; his ideal was to appear in white gloves. Each day brought new bickerings. They made cuts despite my wishes; they left me at the mercy of the insubordination and rudeness of the stage manager and the ballet master, who would not listen to my most modest suggestions. I had to pay the cost of extra musicians in the wings myself. Some stage settings which I wanted for the prologue were declared impossible — I have seen them since in the *Tales of Hoffman*.

Furthermore, the orchestra was very ordinary. There had to be numerous rehearsals which they did not refuse me, but they took advantage of them to spread the report that my music was unplayable. A young journalist who is still alive (I will not name him) wrote two advance notices which were intended to pave the way for the failure of my work.

At the last moment the director saw that he had been on the wrong tack and that he might have a success. As they had played fairyland in the theatre in the Square des-Arts-et-Métiers, he had at hand all the needed material to give me a luxurious stage-setting without great expense. Mlle. Caroline Salla was given the part of Hélène. With her beauty and magnificent voice she was certainly remarkable. But the passages which had been written for the light high soprano of Madame Carvalho were poorly adapted for a dramatic soprano. They concluded, therefore, that I didn't know how to write vocal music.

In spite of everything the work was markedly successful, the natural result of a splendid performance in which two stars — Melchissedech and Mlle. Adeline Théodore, at present teacher of dancing at the Opéra — shone.

Poor Vizentini! His opinion of me has changed greatly since that time. We were made to understand and love each other, so he has become, with years, one of my best and most devoted friends. He first produced my ballet *Javotte* at the Grand-Théâtre in Lyons, which the Monnaie in Brussels had ordered and then refused. He had dreams of directing the Opéra-Comique and installing *Le Timbre d'Argent* there. Fate willed otherwise.

We have seen how the young French school was encouraged under the Empire. The situation has improved and the old state of affairs has never returned. But we find more than the analogy between the old point of view and the one that was revealed not long ago when the French musicians complained that they were more or less sacrificed in favor of their foreign contemporaries. At bottom it is the same spirit in a modified form.

To resume. As everyone knows, the way to become a blacksmith is by working at a forge. Sitting in the shade does not give the experience which develops talent. We should never have known the great days of the Italian theatre, if Rossini, Donizetti, Bellini, and Verdi had had to undergo our régime. If Mozart had had to wait until he was forty to produce his first opera, we should never have had *Don Giovanni* or *Le Nozze di Figaro*, for Mozart died at thirty-five.

The policy imposed on Bizet and Delibes certainly deprived us of several works which would now be among the glories of the repertoire at the Opéra and the Opéra-Comique. That is an irreparable misfortune; one which we cannot sufficiently deplore.

Chapter V

Louis Gallet

As *Déjanire*, cast in a new form, has again appeared in the vast frame of the Opéra stage, I may be allowed to recall my recollections of my friend and collaborator, Louis Gallet, the diligent and chosen companion of my best years, whose support was so dear and precious to me. Collaboration for some reason unknown to me is deprecated. Opera, it is said, should spring from the brain like Minerva, fully armed. So much the better if such divine intellects can be found, but they are rare and always will be. For dramatic and literary art on the one hand and musical art on the other require different powers, which are not ordinarily found in the same person.

I first met Louis Gallet in 1871. Camille du Locle, who was the manager of the Opéra-Comique at the time, could not put on *Le Timbre d'Argent*, and while he waited for better days, which never came, to do that, he offered me a one-act work. He proposed Louis Gallet as my collaborator, although I had not known him until then. "You were made to understand each other," he told me. Gallet was then employed in some capacity at the Beaujon hospital and lived near me in the Faubourg Saint-Honoré. We soon formed the habit of seeing each other every day. Du Locle had judged aright. We had the same tastes in art and literature. We were equally averse to whatever is too theatrical and also to whatever is not sufficiently so, to the commonplace and the too extravagant. We both despised easy success and we understood each other wonderfully. Gallet was not a musician, but he enjoyed and understood music, and he criticised with rare good taste.

Japan had recently been opened to Europeans. Japan was fashionable; all they talked about was Japan, it was a real craze. So the idea of writing a Japanese piece occurred to us. We submitted the idea to du Locle, but he was afraid of an entirely Japanese stage setting. He wanted us to soften the Japanese part, and it was he, I think, who had the idea of making it half Japanese and half Dutch, the way the slight work *La Princesse Jaune* was cast.

That was only a beginning and in our daily talks we sketched the most audacious projects. The leading concerts of the time did not balk at performing large vocal works, as they too often do to-day to the great detriment of the variety of their programmes. We then thought that we were at the beginning of the prosperity of French oratorio which only needed encouragement to flourish. I read by chance in an old Bible this wonderful phrase,

"And it repented the Lord that he had made man on the earth," and so I proposed to Gallet that we do a Deluge. At first he wanted to introduce characters. "No," I said, "put the Bible narrative into simple verse, and I will do the rest." We know with what care and success he accomplished his delicate task. Meanwhile he gave Massenet the texts for *Marie-Madeleine* and *Le Roi de Lahore*, and these two works created a great stir in the operatic world.

We had dreams of historical opera, for we were quite without the prejudice against this form of drama which afflicts the present school. But I was not *persona grata* to the managers and I did not know at what door to knock, when one of my friends, Aimé Gros, took the management of the Grand-Théâtre at Lyons and asked me for a work. This was a fine opportunity and we grasped it. We put together, with difficulty but with infinite zest, our historical opera, *Etienne Marcel*, in which Louis Gallet endeavored to respect as far as is possible in a theatrical work the facts of history. Despite illustrious examples to the contrary he did not believe that it was legitimate to attribute to a character who has actually lived acts and opinions that are entirely fanciful. I was in full agreement with him in that as in so many other things. I go even farther and cannot accustom myself to the queer sauces in which legendary characters are often served. It seems to me that the legend is the interesting thing, and not the character, and that the latter loses all its value when the legend which surrounds it is destroyed. But everyone knows that I am a crank.

Some time after my *Henri VIII*, in which Vaucorbeil had imposed another collaborator on me, Ritt asked me for a new work. We were looking about for a subject, when Gallet came to my house and timidly, as if fearing a rebuff, proposed *Benvenuto Cellini*. I had thought of that for a long time, and the idea had come to me of putting into musical form that fine drama, which had had its hours of glory, where Mélingue modeled the statue of Hebe before the populace. I, therefore, accepted the suggestion with pleasure. This enterprise brought me in touch with Paul Meurice, whom I had known in my childhood, when he was wooing Mlle. Granger, his first wife and an intimate friend of my mother's. Paul Meurice revealed a secret to me: that the romance *Ascanio*, attributed to Alexander Dumas, had been entirely written by Meurice. The work met with a great success, and out of gratitude, Dumas offered to help Meurice in constructing a drama from the romance, which was to be signed by Meurice alone. So it is easy for one who knows Dumas's dramas to find traces of his handiwork in *Benvenuto Cellini*.

It was not particularly easy to make an opera out of the play, and Gallet and I worked together at it with considerable difficulty. We soon saw that we should have to eliminate the famous scene of the casting of the statue. When we reached this point in the play, Benvenuto had already done a good deal of singing, and this scene with its violence seemed certain to exceed the strength of the most valiant artist. In connection with our *Proserpine*, I have been accused of supposing that Vacquerie had genius. It would be too much to say that he had genius, but he certainly had great talent. His prose showed a classical refinement, and his poetry, in spite of fantastic passages which no one could admire, was sonorous in tone, contained precious material, and was both interesting and highly individual. What allured me in *Proserpine* was the amount of inner emotion there was in the drama, which is very advantageous to the music. Music gives expression to feelings which the characters cannot express, and accentuates and develops the picturesqueness of the piece; it makes acceptable what would not even exist without it.

Vacquerie approved highly the convent scene which Gallet invented. This introduced a quiet and peaceful note amidst the violence of the original work. Gallet wrote a sonnet in Alexandrine verse for Sabatino's declaration of his love. I was unable to set this to music, for the twelve feet embarrassed me and prevented my getting into my stride. As I did not know what else to do, I took the sonnet and by main force reduced the verse to ten feet with a cæsura at the fifth foot. I took this to my dear collaborator in fear and trembling, and, as I had feared, he at once fell into the depths of despair.

"That was the best thing in my work," he said. "I nursed and caressed that sonnet, and now you have ruined it."

In the face of this despair, I screwed up my courage. As I had previously cut down the verse, I now tried lengthening out the music. Then, I sang both versions to the disconsolate poet.

And what a miracle! He was altogether reconciled, approved both versions, and did not know which one to choose. We ended with a patchwork. The two quatrains are in verses of ten feet, and the two tiercets in Alexandrine metre.

Outside of our work, too, our relations were delightful. We wrote to each other constantly in both prose and verse; we bombarded each other with sonnets; his letters were sometimes ornamented with water colors, for he drew very well and one of his joys was to cover white paper with color. Gallet drew the sketches for the desert in *Le Roi de Lahore* and the cloister in *Proserpine*.

When Madame Adam founded the *Nouvelle Revue* she offered me the position of musical critic, which I did not think I ought to accept. She did not know where to turn. "Take Gallet," I advised her. "He is an accomplished man of letters. He is not a musician in the sense that he has studied music, but he has the soul of a musician, which is worth much more." Madame Adam followed my advice and found it good.

At this period, under the guise of Wagnerism, the wildest theories and the most extravagant assertions were current in musical criticism. Gallet was naturally well poised and independent and he did not do as the rest did. Instead he opposed them, but from unwillingness to give needless offense he displayed marked tact and discretion in his criticisms. This did him no good, however, for it aroused no sentiment of gratitude, and without giving him credit for a literary style that was rare among librettists, his contemporaries received each of his works with a hostility entirely devoid of either justice or mercy. Gallet felt this hostility keenly. He felt that he did not deserve it, since he took so much care in his work and put so much courtesy into his criticism. The blank verse he used in

Thaïs with admirable regard for color and harmony, counting on the music to take the place of the rhyme, was not appreciated. This verse was free from assonance and the banalities which it draws into operatic works, but it kept the rhythm and sonorous sound which is far removed from prose. That was the period when there was nothing but praise for Alfred Ernst's gibberish, though that was an insult alike to the French language and the masterpieces he had the temerity to translate. Gallet used the same blank verse in *Déjanire,* although its use here was more debatable, but he handled it with surprising skill. Now that this text has been set to music, it shows its full beauty.

Louis Gallet devoted a large part of his time to administrative duties, for he was successively treasurer and manager of hospitals. Nevertheless he produced works in abundance. He left a record of no less than forty operatic librettos, plays, romances, memoirs, pamphlets, and innumerable articles. I wish I knew what to say about the man himself, his unwearying goodness, his loyalty, his scrupulousness, his good humor, his originality, his continual common sense, and his intellect, alert to everything unusual and interesting.

What good talks we used to have as we dined under an arbor in the large garden which was his delight at Lariboisière! I used to take him seeds, and he made amusing botanical experiments with them.

He was seriously ill at one period of his life. He was wonderfully nursed by his wife—who was a saint—and he endured prolonged and atrocious sufferings with the patience of a saint. He watched the growth of his fatal disease with a stoicism worthy of the sages of antiquity and he had no illusion about the implacable illness which slowly but surely would result in his premature death. A constantly increasing deafness was his greatest trouble. This cruel infirmity had made frightful progress when, in 1899, the Arènes de Béziers opened its doors for the second time to *Déjanire.* In spite of everything, including his ill health which made the trip very painful, he wanted to see his work once more. He heard nothing, however—neither the artists, the choruses, nor even the applause of the several thousand spectators who encored it enthusiastically. A little later he passed on, leaving in his friends' hearts and at the work-tables of his collaborators a void which it is impossible to fill.

The First Performance of *Déjanire* at Les Arènes de Béziers

Chapter VI

History and Mythology in Opera

Oceans of ink have been spilled in discussing the question of whether the subjects of operas should be taken from history or mythology, and the question is still a mooted one. To my mind it would have been better if the question had never been raised, for it is of little consequence what the answer is. The only things worth while are whether the music is good and the work interesting. But *Tannhauser*, *Lohengrin*, *Tristan* and *Siegfried* appeared and the question sprang up. The heroes of mythology, we are told, are invested with a prestige which historical characters can never have. Their deeds lose significance and in their place we have their feelings, their emotions, to the great benefit of the operas. After these works, however, *Hans Sachs* (Die Meistersinger) appeared, and although he is not mythical at all he is a fine figure nevertheless. But in this case the plot is of little account, for the interest lies mainly in the emotions—the only thing, it appears, which music with its divine language ought to express.

It is true that music makes it possible to simplify dramatic action and it gives a chance, as well, for the free expression and play of sentiments, emotions and passions. In addition, music makes possible pantomimic scenes which could not be done otherwise, and the music itself flows more easily under such conditions. But that does not mean that such conditions are indispensable for music. Music in its flexibility and adaptability offers inexhaustible resources. Give Mozart a fairy tale like the *Magic Flute* or a lively comedy such as *Le Nozze di Figaro* and he creates without effort an immortal masterpiece.

It is a question whether there is any essential difference between history and mythology. History is made up of what probably happened; mythology of what probably did not happen. There are myths in history and history in myths. Mythology is merely the old form of history. Every myth is rooted in truth. And we have to seek for this truth in the fable, just as we try to reconstruct extinct animals from the remains Time has preserved to us. Behind the story of Prometheus we see the invention of fire; behind the loves of Ceres and Triptolemus the invention of the plow and the beginnings of agriculture. The adventures of the Argonauts show us the first attempts at voyages of exploration and the discovery of gold mines. Volumes have been written about the truths behind the fables, and explanations have been found for the strangest facts of mythology, even for the metamorphoses which Ovid described so poetically.

Halfway between history and mythology come the sacred writings. Each race has its own. Ours are the Old and New Testament. Many believe that these books are myths; a larger number—the Believers—that they are history, Sacred History, the only true history—the only one about which it is not permitted to express a doubt. If you want a proof of this, recall that not so many years ago a clergyman in the Church of England was censured by his ecclesiastical superiors for daring to say in a sermon that the Serpent in the Garden of Eden was symbolical and not a real creature.

And the ecclesiastical authorities were right. The basis of Christianity is the Redemption—the incarnation and sacrifice of God himself to blot out the stain of the first great sin and also to open the Kingdom of Heaven to men. That original sin was Adam's fall, when he followed the example of Eve, a victim of the Serpent's treacherous counsels, and disobeyed the command not to taste the Forbidden Fruit. Eliminate the Garden of Eden, the Serpent, the Forbidden Fruit, and the entire fabric of Christianity crumbles.

If we turn to profane history and take any historical work, we find that the facts are told in such a way that they seem to us beyond dispute. But if we see the same facts from the pen of another historian, we no longer recognize them. The reason is that a writer almost never undertakes the task of wrestling with the giant, History, unless he is impelled to do so by a preconceived idea, by a general conception, or a system he wants to establish. And whether he wants to or not, he sees the facts in a light favorable to his preconceived idea, and observes them through prisms which increase or diminish their importance at his will. Then, however great his discernment and however strong his desire to reach the truth, it is doubtful if he ever will. In history, as elsewhere, absolute truth escapes mankind. Louis XIV, Louis XV, Madame de Maintenon, Madame de Pompadour, Louis XVI, even Napoleon and Josephine, so near our own times, are already quasi-mythical characters. The Louis XIII of *Marion de Lorme* seemed until very lately to be accurate, but recent discoveries show us that he was quite different.

Napoleon III reigned only yesterday, but his picture is already painted in different tints. My entire youth was passed in his reign and my recollections represent him neither as the monster depicted by Victor Hugo nor the kind sympathetic sovereign of present-day stories.

There has been a great deal of discussion of the causes which brought on the War of 1870. We know all that was said and done during the last days of that crisis, but will anyone ever know what was hidden in the minds of the sovereigns, the ministers, and the ambassadors? Will it ever be known whether the Emperor provoked Gramont or Gramont the Emperor? Did they even know themselves? There is one thing the most discerning historian can never reach—the depths of the human soul.

We may, however, learn the secrets of the tomb. It was asserted for a long time that the remains of Voltaire and Rousseau had been exhumed, desecrated, and thrown into the sewers. Victor Hugo wrote a wonderful account of this—an account such as only he could write. One fine day doubt about this occurrence popped up unexpectedly. After waiting a long time it was decided to get to the heart of the matter, and they finally opened the coffins of the two great men. They were peacefully sleeping their last sleep. The deed never took place; its history was a myth.

In this connection Victor Hugo's credulity may be mentioned, for it was astonishing in a man of such colossal genius. He believed in the most incredible things, as the "Man in the Iron Mask," the twin brother of Louis XIV; in the octopus that has no mouth and feeds itself through its arms; and in the reality of the Japanese sirens which the Japanese were said to make out of an ape and a fish. He had some excuse for the sirens as the Académie des Sciences believed in them for a short time.

If what is called history is so near mythology as, many times, to be confounded with it, what about romance and the historical drama in which events, entirely imaginative, must of necessity find a place? What about the long-drawn-out conversations in books and on the stage that are attributed to historical persons? What about the actions attributed to them, which need not be true but only seem to be so? The supernatural element is the only thing lacking to make such works mythological in every way.

Now the supernatural lends itself admirably to expression in music and music finds in the supernatural a wealth of resources. But these resources are by no means indispensable. What music must have above all are emotions and passions laid bare and set in action by what we term the situation. And where can one find more or better situations than in history?

From the time of Lulli until the end of the Eighteenth Century French opera was legendary, that is to say, it was mythological in character and was not, as has been pretended, limited to the depiction of emotion and the inner feelings in order to avoid contingencies. The real motive was to find in fables material for a spectacle. Tragedy, as we know, does not do this, for it can be developed only with considerable difficulty when the stage is crowded with actors. On the contrary, opera, which is free in its movements and can fill a vast stage, seeks for pomp, display and haloes in which gods and goddesses appear, in fact all that can be put into a stage-setting. If they did not use local color, it was because local color had not been invented. Finally, as we all get tired of everything, so they tired of mythology. Then the historical work was adopted and appeared on the stage with success, as is well known. The historical method had no rival until *Robert le Diable* rather timidly brought back the legendary element which triumphed later in the work of Richard Wagner.

In the meantime *Les Huguenots* succeeded *Robert le Diable* and for half a century this was the bright particular star of historical opera. Even now, although its traditions have largely been forgotten and although its workmanship is rather inferior to that of a later time, this memorable work nevertheless shines, like the setting sun, surprisingly brilliantly. The several generations who admired this work were not altogether wrong. There is no necessity to class this brilliant success as a failure, because Robert Schumann, who knew nothing about the stage, denied its worth. It is surprising that Berlioz's judgment has not been set against Schumann's. Berlioz showed his enthusiasm for *Les Huguenots* in his famous treatise on instrumentation.

The great public is little interested in technical polemics and is faithful to the old successes. Although little by little success has come to operas based on legends, there still remains a taste for operas with a historical background. This is not without a reason for as an authoritative critic has said: "A historical drama may contain lyric possibilities far greater than most of the poor, weak mythological librettos on which composers waste their strength, fully persuaded that by doing so they cause 'the holy spirit of Bayreuth to descend upon them.'"

And they never would have dreamed of being mythological, if their god, instead of turning to Scandinavian mythology, had followed his original intention of dramatizing the exploits of Frederick Barbarossa. In his youth he was not opposed to historical opera, for he eulogized *La Musette de Portici*, *La Juive*, and *La Reine de Chypre*. He made some justifiable criticisms of the libretto of the last work, although he admitted that the composer had contrived to write beautiful passages.

"We cannot praise Halévy too highly," he wrote, "for the firmness with which he resists every temptation, to which many of his contemporaries succumb, to steal easy applause by relying blindly on the talent of the singers. On the contrary, he demands that his *virtuosi*, even the most famous of them, shall subordinate themselves to the lofty inspiration of his Muse. He attains this result by the simplicity and truth he knows how to stamp on dramatic melodies."

This is what Richard Wagner said about *La Juive* in 1842.

Fortunately we no longer demand that operas be mythological, for if we did we should have to condemn the famous Russian operas and that is out of the question. However, the method of treatment is still in dispute and this question is involved. One method of treatment is admitted and another is not and it is extremely difficult to tell what is what.

I am now going to do a little special pleading for my *Henri VIII*, which, it would seem, is not in the proper manner. Not that I want to defend the music or to protest against the criticisms it has inspired, for that is not done. But I may, perhaps, be permitted to speak of the piece itself and to tell how the music was adapted to it.

According to the critics it would seem that the whole of *Henri VIII* is superficial and without depth, *en façade*; that the souls of the characters are not revealed, and that the King, at first all sugary sweetness, suddenly becomes a monster without any preparation for, or explanation of, the change.

In this connection let us consider *Boris Godounof,* for there is a historical drama suited to its music. I saw *Boris Godounof* with considerable interest. I heard pleasant and impressive passages, and others less so. In one scene I saw an insignificant friar who suddenly becomes the Emperor in the next scene. One entire act is made up of processions, the ringing of bells, popular songs, and dazzling costumes. In another scene a nurse tells pretty stories to the children in her charge. Then there is a love duet, which is neither introduced nor has any relationship to the development of the work; an incomprehensible evening entertainment, and, finally, funeral scenes in which Chaliapine was admirable. It was not my fault if I did not discover in all that the inner life, the psychology, the introductions, and the explanations which they complain they do not find in *Henri VIII.*

"To Henry VIII," it is stated at the beginning of the work, "nothing is sacred, neither friendship, love nor his word—ill are playthings of his mad whims. He knows neither law nor justice." And when, a little later, smiling, the King hands the holy water to the ambassador he is receiving, the orchestra reveals the working of his mind by repeating the music of the preceding scene. From beginning to end the work is written in this way. But dissertations on such details have not been given the public; the themes of felony, cruelty, and duplicity, and of this and that, have not, as is the fashion of the day, been underlined, so that the critics are excusable for not seeing them.

Not a scene, not a word, they say, shows the soul of Henry VIII. I would like to ask if it is not revealed in the great scene between Henry and Catharine, where he plays with her as a cat with a mouse, where he veils his desire to be rid of her under his religious scruples, and where he heaps on her constantly vile and cruel insinuations, or even in the last scene with its cruel hypocrisies. It is difficult to see why all his passions and all his feelings are not brought into play here. The Russian librettos do no more, nor the operas based on mythology.

But to continue. From the point of view of opera mythology offers one advantage in the use of the miraculous. But the rest of the mythical element offers, rather, difficulties. Characters who never existed and in whom no one believes cannot be made interesting in themselves. They do not sustain, as is sometimes supposed, the music and poetry. On the contrary, the music and poetry give them such reality as they possess. We could not endure the interminable utterances of the mournful Wotan, if it were not for the wonderful music that accompanies them. Orpheus weeping over Eurydice would not move us greatly, if Gluck had not known how to captivate us by his first notes. If it were not for Mozart's music, the puppets of the *Magic Flute* would amount to nothing.

Musicians should, as a matter of fact, be allowed to choose both the subject and motives for their operas according to their temperaments and their feelings. Much youthful talent is lost to-day because the young composers believe that they must obey set rules instead of obeying their own inspiration. All great artists, the illustrious Richard more than any other, mocked the critics.

As I have spoken of Richard Wagner's youth, I will take advantage of the opportunity to reveal a secret of one of his own works which is known to me alone. When Wagner was young, I was a child and I attended constantly the sessions of the Société des Concerts. The kettledrummer of that day had a peculiar habit of breaking in before the rest of the orchestra. When the others began, it produced an effect which the authors had hardly foreseen and which was certain to be condemned. But the effect had a rather distinctive character and I thought it might be possible to use it. Richard Wagner lived in Paris at the time and frequented the famous concerts. There is no doubt that he noted this effect and used it in his overture to *Faust*.

Chapter VII

Art for Art's Sake

What is Art?

Art is a mystery—something which responds to a special sense, peculiar to the human race. This is ordinarily called the esthetic sense, but that is an inexact term, for esthetic sense signifies a sense of the beautiful and what is esthetic is not necessarily beautiful. Sense of style would be better.

Some of the savage races have this sense of style, for their arms and utensils show a remarkable feeling for style, which they lose by contact with civilization.

By art let us understand, if you please, the Fine Arts alone, but including decorative art. Music ought to be included.

I shall astonish most of my readers, when I say that very few people understand music. For most people it is, as Victor Hugo said, an exhalation of art—something for the ear as perfume is for the olfactory sense, a source of vague sensations, necessarily unformed as all sensations are. But musical art is something entirely different. It has line, modeling, color through instrumentation, all making up an ideal sphere where some, like the writer of these lines, live from childhood on, which others attain through education, while many others never know it at all. Furthermore, musical art has more movement than the other fine arts. It is the most mysterious of them all, although the others are mysterious as it is easy to see.

The first manifestation of art occurs through attempts to reproduce objects. Such attempts have been found which date back to prehistoric times. But what is primitive man's idea in such attempts? He wants to record by a line the contour of the object, the likeness of which he wishes to preserve. This contour and this line do not exist in nature. The whole philosophy of art is in that crude drawing. It bases itself on nature even while making something quite different in response to a special, inexplicable need of the human spirit. Accordingly nothing can be more chimerical or vain than the advice so often given to the artist to be truthful. Art can never be true, even though it should not be false. It should be true artistically, by giving an artistic translation which will satisfy the sense of style of which we have spoken. When Art has satisfied this sense of style, the object of artistic expression has been attained; nothing more can be asked. But it is not the "vain effort of an unproductive cleverness," as our M. de Mun has said; it is an effort to satisfy a legitimate need, one of the loftiest and most honorable in human nature — the need of art.

If this is so, why should we demand that Art be useful or moral? It is both in its own way, for it awakens noble and honest sentiments in the soul. That was the opinion of Théophile Gautier, but Victor Hugo disagreed. The sun is beautiful, he used to say, and it is useful. That is true, but the sun is not an object of art. Besides, how many times Victor Hugo denied his own doctrine by writing verses which were merely brilliant descriptions or admirable bits of imagination?

We are, however, talking of art and not of literature. Literature becomes art in poetry but forsakes it in prose. Even if some of the great prose writers rendered their prose artistic through the beauty and harmony of their periods and the picturesqueness of their expressions, still prose is not art in its real nature. So, crude indecency aside, what would be immoral in prose ceases to be immoral in verse, for in poetry Art follows its own code and form transcends the subject matter. That is why a great poet, Sully-Prudhomme, preferred prose to verse when he wanted to write philosophically, for he feared, on account of the superiority of form to substance in poetry, that his ideas would not be taken seriously. That explains as well why parents take young girls to hear an opera, when if the same piece was played without music they would be appalled at the idea. What Christian is ever shocked by *La Juive* or Catholic frightened away from *Les Huguenots*?

Because prose is far removed from art, it is unsuited to music, despite the fact that this ill-assorted union is fashionable to-day? In poetry there has been an effort to make it so artistic that form alone is considered and verse is written which is entirely without sense. But that is a fad which can't last long.

Sometime ago M. de Mun said:

"Not to take sides is what the author is inhibited from doing. Art, to my way of thinking, is a setting forth of ideas. If it is not that—if it limits itself solely to considerations of form, to a worship of beauty for its own sake, without regard to the deeds and thoughts it brings to light, then it seems to me no better than the vain effort of an unproductive cleverness."

The eminent speaker is absolutely right as far as prose is concerned, but we cannot agree with him if poetry is considered.

Victor Hugo, in his marvellous ode, *La Lyre et La Harpe* brings Paganism and Christianity face to face. Each speaks in turn, and the poet in his last stanza seems to acknowledge that both are right, but that does not prevent the ode from being a masterpiece. That would not be possible in prose, but in the poem the poetry carries all before it.

M. Saint-Saëns in his Later Years

Why is it that geniuses like Victor Hugo, distinguished minds, thinkers, and profound critics, refuse to see that Art is a special entity which responds to a certain sense? If Art accommodates itself marvellously, if it accords itself with the precepts of morality and passion, it is nevertheless sufficient unto itself—and in its self-sufficiency lies its heights of greatness.

The first prelude of Sebastian Bach's *Wohltemperirte Klavier* expresses nothing, and yet that is one of the marvels of music. The Venus de Milo expresses nothing, and it is one of the marvels of sculpture.

To tell the truth, it is proper to add that in order not to be immoral Art must appeal to those who have a feeling for it. Where the artist sees only beautiful forms, the gross see only nudity. I have seen a good man scandalized at the sight of Ingres's *La Source*.

Just as morality has no function to be artistic, so Art has nothing to do with morality. Both have their own functions, and each is useful in its own way. The final aim of morality is morality; of art, art, and nothing else.

Chapter VIII

Popular Science and Art

René Bazin has sketched cleverly Pasteur's brilliant career. France has no clearer claim to glory than in Pasteur, for he is one of the men, who, in spite of everything, keeps her in the first rank of nations.

A rare good fortune attended him. While many scholars who seek the truth without concerning themselves with the practical results have to wait many long years before their discoveries can be used, Pasteur's discoveries were useful at once. So the mob, which cannot understand science studied for its own sake, appreciated Pasteur's works. He saved millions to the public treasury, and tens of thousands of human lives.

He had already secured a notable place in science when the public learned his name through the memorable contest between him and Pouchet over "spontaneous generation." The probabilities of the case were on Pouchet's side. People refused to believe that these organisms which developed in great numbers in an enclosed jar or that the molds which developed under certain conditions were not produced spontaneously. The youth of the time went wild over the question.

I was constantly being asked, "Are you for Pouchet or Pasteur?" and my invariable response was, "I shall be for the one who proves he is right." I was unwilling to admit that any such question could be solved *a priori* in accordance with preconceived ideas, although I must confess that among my friends I found no one of the same opinion.

We know how Pasteur won a striking victory through his patience and his genius. He demonstrated that millions and millions of germs are present in the air about us and that when one of them finds favorable conditions, a living being appears which engenders others. "Many are called, but few are chosen." This law may seem unjust, but it is one of the great laws of Nature.

Pasteur, the great benefactor, whose discoveries did so much for all classes of society, should have been popular, but he was, on the contrary, extremely unpopular. The leading publicists of the day were influenced by some inexplicable sentiment and they made constant war on him. When, after several years of prodigious labor, Pasteur ventured to assert himself, they took advantage of his following the dictates of humanity in accepting all sorts of cases, curable or not, to spread a report that his treatment did not cure, but instead gave the disease which it was supposed to cure. Popular fury was aroused to such a height, that a monster mass meeting was held *against* Pasteur. Louise Michel addressed this meeting with her customary vigor of speech and amidst frantic applause shouted this unqualified remark, "*Scientific questions should be settled by the people.*"

By this time everybody was talking about microbes, and a shop on the boulevards announced an exhibition of them. They used what is known as a solar microscope and threw on a screen, suitably enlarged, the animalculae which grow in impure water, the larvae of mosquitoes, and other insects, which bear about the same relation to microbes that an elephant does to a flea. I went into this establishment, and saw the plain people with their wives looking at the exhibition very seriously and really believing that they saw the famous microbes. One of them near me said, with a knowing air, "What won't science do next?"

I was indignant, and I had all I could do to keep from saying: "They are fooling you. What they are showing you is not Science, at the most only its antechamber. As for you who are deceiving these naïve good people, you are only impostors."

But I kept still; I would only have succeeded in getting thrown out. But I said to myself—and I still say—"Why not enlighten these people, who obviously want light?" It is impossible to *teach* them science, but it should be possible to make them at least comprehend what science *is*, for they have no idea of it now. They do not know—in this era when they are constantly talking about their rights and urged to demand more wages and less work—that there are young people who are spending their best years and leading a precarious existence, working day and night, without hope of personal profit, with no other end in view besides the hope of discovering new facts from which humanity may benefit at some time in the future. They do not know that all the benefits of civilization which they carelessly enjoy are the result of the long, painful and enormous work of the thinkers whom they regard as idlers and visionaries who grow rich from the sweat of the toilers. In a word, they should be taught to give respect to what is worthy of it.

It is true that there are scientific congresses, but these are serious gatherings which attract only the select few. It should be possible to interest everybody, and in order to make scientific meetings interesting we should use motion pictures and concerts.

But here we trench on art. We ought to teach the people not only science but art as well, but the latter is the more difficult.

Modern peoples are not artistic. The Greeks were, and the Japanese were, before the European invasion. An artistic people is recognized by their ignorance of "objects of art," for in such an environment art is everywhere. An artistic people no more dreams of creating art than a great nobleman of consciously exhibiting a distinguished manner. Distinction lies in his slightest mannerism without his being conscious of the fact. So, among artistic peoples, the most ordinary and humble objects have style. And this style, furthermore, is in perfect harmony with the purpose of the object. It is absolutely appropriate for that purpose in its proportions, in the purity of its lines, the elegance of its form, its perfection of execution, and, above all, in its meaning. When an outcry is raised against the ugliness and tawdriness of certain objects in this country, the answer is, "But see how cheap they are!" But style and conscience in work cost nothing. Feeling for art is, however, inherent in human nature. The weapons of primitive peoples are beautiful. The prehistoric hatchets of the Stone Age are perfect in their contours. There is, therefore, no question of creating a feeling for art in the people, but of awakening it.

Music holds so important a place in the modern world, that we ought to begin with that. There is plenty of gay music, easy to understand, which is in harmony with the laws of art, and the people ought to hear it instead of the horrors which they cram into our ears under the pretence of satisfying our tastes. What pleases people most is sentimental music, but it need not be a silly sentimentality. Instead, they ought to give the people the charming airs which grow, as naturally as daisies on a lawn, in the vast field of opéra-comique. That is not high art, it is true, but it is pretty music and it is high art compared with what is heard too often in the cafés. I am not ignorant of the fact that such establishments employ talented people. But along with the good, what frightful things one hears! And no one would listen to their instrumental repertoire anywhere else!

Every time anyone has tried to raise the standards and employ real singers and real *virtuosi*, the attendance has increased. But, very often, even at the theatres, the managers satisfy their own tastes under the pretence of satisfying that of the public. That is, of course, intensely human. We judge others by ourselves.

A famous manager once said to me, as he pointed to an empty house, "The public is amazing. Give them what they like, and they don't come!"

One day I was walking in a garden. There was a bandstand and musicians were playing some sort of music. The crowd was indifferent and passed by talking without paying the slightest attention. Suddenly there sounded the first notes of the delightful *andante* of Beethoven's *Symphony in D*—a flower of spring with a delicate perfume. At the first notes all walking and talking stopped. And the crowd stood motionless and in an almost religious silence as it listened to the marvel. When the piece was over, I went out of the garden, and near the entrance I heard one of the managers say,

"There, you see they don't like that kind of music."

And that kind of music was never played there again.

Chapter IX

Anarchy in Music

Music is as old as human nature. We can get some idea of what it was at first from the music of savage tribes. There were a few notes and rudimentary melodies with blows struck in cadence as an accompaniment; or, sometimes, the same primitive rhythms without any accompaniment—and nothing else! Then melody was perfected and the rhythms became more complicated. Later came Greek music, of which we know little, and the music of the East and Far East.

Music, as we now understand the term, began with the attempts at harmony in the Middle Ages. These attempts were labored and difficult, and the uncertainty of their gropings, combined with the slowness of their development, excites our wonder. Centuries were necessary before the writing of music became exact, but, slowly, laws were elaborated. Thanks to them the works of the Sixteenth Century came into being, in all their admirable purity and learned polyphony. Hard and inflexible laws engendered an art analogous to primitive painting. Melody was almost entirely absent and was relegated to dance tunes and popular songs. But the dance tunes of the time, on which, perhaps, erudition was not used sufficiently, were written in the same polyphonic style and with the same rigid correctness as the madrigals and the church music.

We know that the popular songs found their way into the church music and that Palestrina's great reform consisted in banishing them. However, we should get but a feeble idea of the part they played, if we imagined that they naturally belonged there. Take a well known air, *Au Claire de la Lune*, for example, and make each note a whole note sung by the tenor, while the other voices dialogue back and forth in counterpoint, and see what is left of the song for the listener. The scandal of *La Messe de l'Homme armé* was entirely theoretical.

We simply do not know how they played these anthems, masses, and madrigals, in the absence of any indication of either the time or the emphasis. We find a few directions for expression, as in the first measures of Palestrina's *Stabat Mater* but such directions are extremely rare. They are simply the first signs of the dawn of the far-off day of music with expression. Certain learned and well-intentioned persons endeavor to compare this music with ours, and we surprise in some of the modern editions instances of *molto expressivo* which seem to be good guesses. This exclusively consonant music, in which the intervals of fourths were considered dissonant, while the diminishing fifth was the *diabolus in musica*, ought from its very nature to be antithetical to expression. Nothing in the *Kyrie*, in *La Messe du Pape Marcel*, gives the impression of a prayer, unless expressive accents, without any real justification, are introduced by main strength.

Expression came into existence with the chord of the dominant seventh from which all modern harmony developed. This invention is attributed to Monteverde. No matter what has been said, however, it occurs in Palestrina's *Adoremus*. Floods of ink have been poured out in discussing this question, some affirming, while others — and not the least, by any manner of means — denying the existence of the famous chord. No equivocation is possible. It is a simultaneously played chord held by four voices for a whole measure. What is certain is that Palestrina, by putting aside the rules, made a discovery, the significance of which he did not realize.

With the introduction of the seventh interval a new era began. It would be a grave error to believe that the rules were overturned, for, instead, new principles were added to old ones as new conditions demanded. They learned how to modulate, how to transpose from one key to the next key and finally to the keys farthest away. In his treatise on harmony Fétis studied this evolution in a masterly manner. Unfortunately his scholarship was not combined with deep musical feeling. For example, he saw faults in Mozart and Beethoven where there are only beauties, and beauties which even an ignorant listener — if he is naturally musical — will see without trouble. He did not understand the vast difference between the unlettered person who commits a solecism and Pascal, the inventor of a new syntax.

However that may be, Fétis gave us a comprehensive review in broad outlines of musical evolution down to what he justly called the "omnitonic system," which Richard Wagner has achieved since. "Beyond that," he said, "I can see nothing more."

He did not foresee the a-tonic system, but that is what we have come to. There is no longer any question of adding to the old rules new principles which are the natural expression of time and experience, but simply of casting aside all rules and every restraint.

"Everyone ought to make his own rules. Music is free and unlimited in its liberty of expression. There are no perfect chords, dissonant chords or false chords. All aggregations of notes are legitimate."

That is called, and they believe it, the *development of taste.*

He whose taste is developed by this system is not like the man who by tasting a wine can tell you its age and its vineyard, but he is rather like the fellow who with perfect indifference gulps down good or bad wine, brandy or whiskey, and prefers that which burns his gullet the most. The man who gets his work hung in the Sâlon is not the one who puts on his canvas delicate touches in harmonious tones, but he who juxtaposes vermillion and Veronese green. The man with a "developed taste" is not the one who knows how to get new and unexpected results by passing from one key to another, as the great Richard did in *Die Meistersinger*, but rather the man who abandons all keys and piles up dissonances which he neither introduces nor concludes and who, as a result, grunts his way through music as a pig through a flower garden.

Possibly they may go farther still. There seems to be no reason why they should linger on the way to untrammeled freedom or restrict themselves within a scale. The boundless empire of sound is at their disposal and let them profit by it. That is what dogs do when they bay at the moon, cats when they meow, and the birds when they sing. A German has written a book to prove that the birds sing false. Of course he is wrong for they do not sing false. If they did, their song would not sound agreeable to us. They sing outside of scales and it is delightful, but that is not man-made art.

Some Spanish singers give a similar impression, through singing interminable grace notes beyond notation. Their art is intermediate between the singing of the birds and of man. It is not a higher art.

In certain quarters they marvel at the progress made in the last thirty years. The architects of the Fifteenth Century must have reasoned in the same way. They did not appreciate that they were assassinating Gothic art, and that after some centuries we would have to revert to the art of the Greeks and Romans.

Chapter X

The Organ

When hairy Pan joined reeds of different lengths and so invented the flute which bears his name, he was, in reality, creating the organ. It needed only to add to this flute a keyboard and bellows to make one of those pretty instruments the first painters used to put in the hands of angels. As it developed and gradually became the most grandiose of the instruments, the organ, with its depth of tone modified and increased tenfold by the resonance of the great cathedrals, took on its religious character.

The organ is more than a single instrument. It is an orchestra, a collection of the pipes of Pan of every size, from those as small as a child's playthings to those as gigantic as the columns of a temple. Each one corresponds to what is termed an organ-stop. The number is unlimited.

The Romans made organs which must have been simple from the musical standpoint, though they were complicated in their mechanical construction. They were called hydraulic organs. The employment of water in a wind instrument has greatly perplexed the commentators. Cavaillé-Coll studied the question and solved the problem by demonstrating that the water compressed the air. This system was ingenious but imperfect, since it was applicable only to the most primitive instruments. The keys, it seems, were very large, and were struck by blows of the fist.

Let us leave erudition for art and primitive for perfected instruments. By the time of Sebastian Bach and Rameau the organ had taken on its grandiose character. The stops had multiplied and the organist *called* them by means of registers which he drew out or pushed back at will. In order to give greater resources, the builder multiplied the keyboards. Pedals were introduced to help out the keyboards. At that time Germany alone had pedals worthy of the name and worth while in playing an interesting bass part. In France and elsewhere the rudimentary pedals were only used for certain fundamental notes or in prolonged *tenutos*. No one outside of Germany could play Sebastian Bach's compositions.

Playing on the old instruments was fatiguing and uncomfortable. The touch was heavy and, when one used both the pedals and the keyboards, a real display of strength was necessary. A similar display was necessary to draw out or push back the registers, some of which were beyond the player's reach. In short, an assistant was necessary, in fact several assistants in playing large organs like those at Harlem or Arnheim in Holland. It was almost impossible to modify the combinations of stops. All nuances, save the abrupt change from strong to soft and vice versa, were impossible.

It remained for Cavaillé-Coll to change all this and open up new fields of usefulness for the organ. He introduced in France keyboards worthy of the name, and he gave to the higher notes, through his invention of harmonic stops, a brilliancy they had lacked. He invented wonderful combinations which allow the organist to change his combinations and to vary the tone, without the aid of an assistant and without leaving the keyboard. Even before his day a scheme had been devised of enclosing certain stops in a box protected by shutters which a pedal opened and closed at will; this permitted the finest shadings. By different processes the touch of the organ was made as delicate as that of the piano.

For some years the Swiss organ-makers have been inventing new facilities which make the organist a sort of magician. The manifold resources of the marvellous instrument are at his command, obedient to his slightest wish.

These resources are prodigious. The compass of the organ far surpasses that of all the instruments of the orchestra. The violin notes alone reach the same height, but with little carrying power. As for the lower tones, there is no competitor of the thirty-two-foot pipes, which go two octaves below the violoncello's low C. Between the *pianissimo* which almost reaches the limit where sound ceases and silence begins, down to a range of formidable and terrifying power, every degree of intensity can be obtained from this magical instrument. The variety of its timbre is broad. There are flute stops of various kinds; tonal stops that approximate the timbre of stringed instruments; stops for effecting changes in which each note, formed from several pipes, bring out simultaneously its fundamental and harmonic sounds; stops which serve to imitate the instruments of the orchestra, such as the trumpet, the clarinet, and the cremona (an obsolete instrument with a timbre peculiar to itself) and the bassoon. There are celestial voices of several kinds, produced by combinations of two simultaneous stops which are not tuned in perfect unison. Then we have the famous *Vox Humana*, a favorite with the public, which is alluring even though it is tremulous and nasal, and we have the innumerable combinations of all these different stops, with the gradations that may be obtained through indefinite commingling of the tones of this marvellous palette.

Add to all this the continual breathing of the monster's lungs which gives the sounds an incomparable and inimitable steadiness. Human beings were used for a long time to fill these lungs—blowers working away with hands and feet. We do much better now. The great organ in Albert Hall, London, is supplied with air by steam which assures the organist an inexhaustible supply. Other instruments use gas engines which are more manageable. Then, there is the hydraulic system, which is very powerful and easily used, for one has only to pull out a plug to set the bellows in motion.

These mechanical systems, however, are not entirely free from accidents. I discovered that fact when I was concluding the first part of the *Adagio* in Liszt's great *Fantaisie* in the beautiful Victoria Hall in Geneva. The pipe which brought in the water burst and the organ was mute. I have always thought, perhaps wrongly, that malice had something to do with the accident.

This Liszt *Fantaisie* is the most extraordinary piece for the organ there is. It lasts forty minutes and the interest is sustained throughout. Just as Mozart in his *Fantaisie et Sonate in C minor* foresaw the modern piano, so Liszt, writing this *Fantaisie* more than half a century ago, appears to have foreseen the instrument of a thousand resources which we have to-day.

Let us have the courage to admit, however, that these resources are only partly utilized as they can or should be. To draw from a great instrument all its possibilities, to begin with, one must understand it thoroughly, and that understanding cannot be gained over night. The organ, as we have seen, is a collection of an indefinite number of instruments. It places before the organist extraordinary means of expressing himself. No two of these instruments are precisely alike. The organ is only a theme with innumerable variations, determined by the place in which it is to be installed, by the amount of money at the builder's disposal, by his inventiveness, and, often, by his personal whims. As a result time is required for the organist to learn his instrument thoroughly. After this he is as free as the fish in the sea, and his only preoccupation is the music. Then, to play freely with the colors on his vast palette, there is but one way—he must plunge boldly into improvisation.

Now improvisation is the particular glory of the French school, but it has been injured seriously of late by the influence of the German school. Under the pretext that an improvisation is not so good as one of Sebastian Bach's or Mendelssohn's masterpieces, young organists have stopped improvising.

That point of view is harmful because it is absolutely false; it is simply the negation of eloquence. Consider what the legislative hall, the lecture room and the court would be like if nothing but set pieces were delivered. We are familiar with the fact that many an orator and lawyer, who is brilliant when he talks, becomes dry as dust when he tries to write. The same thing happens in music. Lefébure-Wély was a wonderful improviser (I can say this emphatically, for I heard him) but he left only a few unimportant compositions for the organ. I might also name some of my contemporaries who express themselves completely only through their improvisations. The organ is thought-provoking. As one touches the organ, the imagination is awakened, and the unforeseen rises from the depths of the unconscious. It is a world of its own, ever new, which will never be seen again, and which comes out of the darkness, as an enchanted island comes from the sea.

Instead of this fairyland, we too often see only some of Sebastian Bach's or Mendelssohn's pieces repeated continuously. The pieces themselves are very fine, but they belong to concerts and are entirely out of place in church services. Furthermore, they were written for old instruments and they apply either not at all, or badly, to the modern organ. Yet there are those who think this belief spells progress.

I am fully aware of what may be said against improvisation. There are players who improvise badly and their playing is uninteresting. But many preachers speak badly. That, however, has nothing to do with the real issue. A mediocre improvisation is always endurable, if the organist has grasped the idea that church music should harmonize with the service and aid meditation and prayer. If the organ music is played in this spirit and results in harmonious sounds rather than in precise music which is not worth writing out, it still is comparable with the old glass windows in which the individual figures can hardly be distinguished but which are, nevertheless, more charming than the finest modern windows. Such an improvisation may be better than a fugue by a great master, on the principle that nothing in art is good unless it is in its proper place.

The Madeleine where M. Saint-Saëns played the organ for twenty years

During the twenty years I played the organ at the Madeleine, I improvised constantly, giving my fancy the widest range. That was one of the joys of life.

But there was a tradition that I was a severe, austere musician. The public was led to believe that I played nothing but fugues. So current was this belief that a young woman about to be married begged me to play no fugues at her wedding!

Another young woman asked me to play funeral marches. She wanted to cry at her wedding, and as she had no natural inclination to do so, she counted on the organ to bring tears to her eyes.

But this case was unique. Ordinarily, they were afraid of my severity—although this severity was tempered.

One day one of the parish vicars undertook to instruct me on this point. He told me that the Madeleine audiences were composed in the main of wealthy people who attended the Opéra-Comique frequently, and formed musical tastes which ought to be respected.

"Monsieur l'abbé," I replied, "when I hear from the pulpit the language of opéra-comique, I will play music appropriate to it, and not before!"

Chapter XI

Joseph Haydn and the "Seven Words"

Joseph Haydn, that great musician, the father of the symphony and of all modern music, has been neglected. We are too prone to forget that concerts are, in a sense, museums in which the older schools of music should be represented. Music is something besides a source of sensuous pleasure and keen emotion, and this resource, precious as it is, is only a chance corner in the wide realm of musical art. He who does not get absolute pleasure from a simple series of well-constructed chords, beautiful only in their arrangement, is not really fond of music. The same is true of the one who does not prefer the first prelude of the *Wohltemperirte Klavier*, played without gradations, just as the author wrote it for the harpsichord, to the same prelude embellished with an impassioned melody; or who does not prefer a popular melody of character or a Gregorian chant without any accompaniment to a series of dissonant and pretentious chords.

The directors of great concerts should love music themselves and should lead the public to appreciate it. They should not allow the masters to be forgotten, for their only fault was that they were not born in our times and they never dreamed of attempting to satisfy the tastes of an unborn generation. Above all, the directors should grant recognition to masters like Joseph Haydn who were in advance of their own times and who seem now and then to belong to our own.

The only examples of Joseph Haydn's immense work that the present generation knows are two or three symphonies, rarely and perfunctorily performed. This is the same as saying that we do not know him at all. No musician was ever more prolific or showed a greater wealth of imagination. When we examine this mine of jewels, we are astonished to find at every step a gem which we would have attributed to the invention of some modern or other. We are dazzled by their rays, and where we expect black-and-whites we find pastels grown dim with time.

Of Haydn's one hundred and eighteen symphonies, many are simple trifles written from day to day for Prince Esterhazy's little chapel, when the master was musical director there. But after Haydn was called to London by Salomon, a director of concerts, where he had a large orchestra at his disposal, his genius took magnificent flights. Then he wrote great symphonies and in them the clarinets for the first time unfolded the resources from which the modern orchestra has profited so abundantly. Originally the clarinet played a humble rôle, as the name indicates. *Clarinetto* is the diminutive of *clarino*, and the instrument was invented to replace the shrill tones that the trumpet lost as it gained in depth of tone.

Old editions of Haydn's symphonies show a picturesque arrangement, in that the disposition of the orchestra is shown on the printed page. Above, is a group made up of drums and the brass. In the center is a second group—the flutes, oboes and bassoons, while the stringed instruments are at the bottom of the page. When clarinets are used, they are a part of the first group. This pretty arrangement has, unfortunately, not been followed in the modern editions of these symphonies. In the works written in London the clarinet has utterly forgotten its origins. It has left the somewhat plebeian world of the brasses and has gained admittance to the more refined society of the woods. Haydn, in his first attempts, took advantage of the beautiful heavy tones, "*chalumeau*," and the flexibility and marvellous range of a beautiful instrument.

During his stay in London Haydn sketched an *Orfeo* which he never completed, as the theatre which ordered it failed before it was finished. Only fragments of the work remain, and, fortunately enough, these have been engraved in an orchestra score. These fragments are uneven in value. The dialogue, or recitative, which should bind them together was lost and so we are unable to judge them fairly. Among the fragments is a brilliant aria on Eurydice which is rather ridiculous, while another on Eurydice dying is charming. We also find music for mysterious *English horns*; it is written as for clarinets in B flat and reaches heights which are impossible for the instrument we now know as the English horn. There is also a beautiful bass part. This has been provided with Latin words and is sung in churches. This aria was assigned to a Creon who does not appear in the other fragments. One scene shows Eurydice running up and down the banks pursued by demons. Another depicts the death of Orpheus, killed by the Bacchantes. This score is a curiosity and nothing more, and a reading causes no regret that the work was not completed.

Like Gluck, Joseph Haydn had the rare advantage of developing constantly. He did not reach the height of his genius until an age when the finest faculties are, ordinarily, in a decline. He astounded the musical world with his *Creation*, in which he displayed a fertility of imagination and a magnificence of orchestral richness that the oratorio had never known before. Emboldened by his success he wrote the *Seasons*, a colossal work, the most varied and the most picturesque in the history of ancient or modern music. In this instance the oratorio is no longer entirely religious. It gives an audacious picture of nature with realistic touches which are astonishing even now. There is an artistic imitation of the different sounds in nature, as the rustling of the leaves, the songs of the birds in the woods and on the farm, and the shrill notes of the insects. Above all that is the translation into music of the profound emotions to which the different aspects of nature give birth, as the freshness of the forests, the stifling heat before a storm, the storm itself, and the wonderful sunset that follows. Then there is a huntsman's chorus which strikes an entirely different note. There are grape harvests, with the mad dances that follow them. There is the winter, with a poignant introduction which reminds us of pages in Schumann. But be reassured, the author does not leave us to the rigors of the cold. He takes us into a farmhouse where the women are spinning and where the peasants are drawn about the fire, listening to a funny tale and laughing immoderately with a gaiety which has never been surpassed.

But this gigantic work does not end without giving us a glimpse of Heaven, for with one grand upward burst of flight, Haydn reaches the realms where Handel and Beethoven preceded him. He equals them and ends his picture in a dazzling blaze of light.

This is the sort of work of which the public remains in ignorance and which it ought to know.

But all this is not what I started out to say. I wanted to write about a delicate, touching, reserved and precious work by the same author—*The Seven Words of Christ on the Cross*. This work has appeared in three forms—for an orchestra and chorus, for an orchestra alone, and for a quartet. When I was a young man, they used to say in Paris that this work was originally written for a quartet, then developed for an orchestra, and, finally, the voices were added.

Chance took me to Cadiz, once upon a time, and there I was given the true story of this beautiful piece of work. To my astonishment I learned that it had been first performed in the city of Cadiz. They even spoke of a competition in which Haydn won the prize, but there was never any such contest. The work was ordered from the author, but the question is who ordered it. Two religious circles, the Cathedral and the Cueva del Rosario, both lay claim to the initiative. I have gone over all the evidence in this dispute which is of little interest to us, for the only interest is the origin of the composition. There is not the slightest doubt that the *Seven Words* was written in the first place for an orchestra in 1785, and its destination, as we shall see, was settled by the author himself.

In his *Memoires pour la Biographie et la Bibliographie de l'ile de Cadix*, Don Francisco de Miton, Marquis de Meritos, relates that he corresponded with Haydn and ordered this composition which was to be performed at the Cathedral in Cadiz. According to his account Haydn said that "the composition was due more to what Señor Milton wrote than to his own invention, for it showed every motif so marvellously that on reading the instructions he seemed to read the music itself."

If the Marquis was not boasting, we must confess that the ingenuous Haydn was not so ingenuous as has been thought, and that he knew how to flatter his patrons.

In 1801 Breitkopf and Haertel published the work with the addition of the vocal parts at Leipzig. This edition had a preface by the author in which he said:

> About fifteen years ago, a curé at Cadiz engaged
> me to write some passages of instrumental music
> on the Seven Words of Christ on the Cross. It was
> the custom at that time to play an oratorio at the
> Cathedral during Holy Week, and they took great
> pains to give as much solemnity as possible. The

walls, the windows and the pillars of the church were hung in black, and only a single light in the centre shone in the sanctuary. The doors were closed at mid-day and the orchestra began to play. After the opening ceremonies the bishop entered the pulpit, pronounced one of the "Seven Words" and delivered a few words inspired by it. Then he descended, knelt before the altar, and remained there for some time. This pause was relieved by the music. The bishop ascended and descended six times more and each time, after his homily, music was played. My music was to be adapted to these ceremonies.

The problem of writing seven *adagios* to be performed consecutively, each one to last ten minutes, without wearying the audience, was not an easy one to solve, and I soon recognized the impossibility of making my music conform to the prescribed limits.

The work was written and printed without words. Later the opportunity of adding them was offered, so the oratorio which Breitkopf and Haertel publish to-day is a complete work and, so far as the vocal part is concerned, entirely new.

The kind reception which it has received among amateurs makes me hope that the entire public will welcome it with the same kindness.

Haydn feared to weary his hearers. Our modern bards have no such vain scruple.

Michel Haydn, Joseph's brother and the author of some highly esteemed religious compositions, has been generally credited with the addition of the vocal parts to the *Seven Words*. Joseph Haydn did not say that this was the case, but it would seem that if he did the work himself he would have said so in his preface.

This vocal part, however, adds nothing to the value of the work. And it is of no great consequence who the author of the arrangement for the quartet was. At the time there were many amateurs who played on stringed instruments. They used to meet frequently and everything in music was arranged for quartets just as now everything is arranged for piano duets. Some of Beethoven's sonatas were arranged in this form. The piano killed the quartet, and it is a great pity, for the quartet is the purest form of instrumental music. It is the first form—the fountain of Hippocrene. Now instrumental music drinks from every cup and the result is that many times it seems drunk.

To return to the *Seven Words*. Their symphonic form is the only one worth considering. They are eloquent enough without the aid of voices, for their charm penetrates. Unlike the *Creation* and the *Seasons* they do not demand extraordinary means of execution, and nothing is easier than to give them.

The opera houses are closed on Good Friday, and it used to be the custom to give evening concerts, vaguely termed "Sacred Concerts," because their programmes were made up wholly or in part of religious music. This good custom has disappeared and with it the opportunity to give the public such delightful works as the *Seven Words*, and so many other things which harmonize with the character of the day.

At one of these Sacred Concerts, Pasdeloup presented on the same evening the *Credo* from Liszt's *Missa Solemnis* and the one from Cherubini's *Messe du Sacre*. Liszt's *Credo* was received with a storm of hisses, while Cherubini's was praised to the skies. I could not help thinking—I was somewhat unjust, for Cherubini's work has merit—of the people of Jerusalem who acclaimed Barrabas and demanded the crucifixion of Jesus.

To-day Liszt's *Credo* is received with wild applause—Victor Hugo did his part-while Cherubini's is never revived.

Chapter XII

The Liszt centenary was celebrated everywhere with elaborate festivities, perhaps most notably at Budapest where the *Missa Solemnis* was sung in the great cathedral—that alone would have been sufficient glory for the composer. At Weimar, which, during his lifetime, Liszt made a sort of musical Mecca, they gave a performance of his deeply charming oratorio *Die Legende von der Heiligen Elisabeth*. The festival at Heidelberg was of special interest as it was organized by the General Association of German Musicians which Liszt had founded fifty years before. Each year this society gives in a different city a festival which lasts several days. It admits foreign members and I was once a member as Berlioz's successor on Liszt's own invitation. Disagreements separated us, and I had had no relation with the society for a number of years when they asked me to take part in this festival. A refusal would have been misunderstood and I had to accept, although the idea of performing at my age alongside such *virtuosi* as Risler, Busoni, and Friedheim, in the height of their talent, was not encouraging.

The festival lasted four days and there were six concerts—four with the orchestra and a chorus. They gave the oratorio *Christus*, an enormous work which takes up all the time allowed for one concert; the Dante and Faust symphonies, and the symphonic poems *Ce qu'on entend sur la montagne* and *Tasso*, to mention only the most important works.

The oratorio *Christus* lacks the fine unity of the *Saint Elisabeth*. But the two works are alike in being divided into a series of separate episodes. While the different episodes in *Saint Elisabeth* solve the difficult problem of creating variety and retaining unity, the parts of *Christus* are somewhat unrelated. There is something for every taste. Certain parts are unqualifiedly admirable; others border on the theatrical; still others are nearly or entirely liturgical, while, finally, some are picturesque, although there are some almost confusing. Like Gounod, Liszt was sometimes deceived and attributed to ordinary and simple sequences of chords a profound significance which escaped the great majority of his hearers. There are some pages of this sort in *Christus*.

But there are beautiful and wonderful things in this vast work. If we regret that the author lingered too long in his imitation of the *Pifferari* of the Roman campagna, on the other hand, we are delighted by the symphonic interlude *Les Bergers à la Crèche*. It is very simple, but in an inimitable simplicity of taste which is the secret of great artists alone. It is surprising that this interlude does not appear in the repertoire of all concerts.

The Dante symphony has not established itself in the repertoires as has the Faust symphony. It was performed for the first time in Paris at a concert I organized and managed at a time when Liszt's works were distrusted. Along with the Dante symphony we had the Andante (Gretchen) from the Faust symphony, the symphonic poem *Fest Kloenge*, a charming work which is never played now, and still other works. It would be hard to imagine all the opposition I had to overcome in giving that concert. There was the hostility of the public, the ill-will of the Théâtre-Italien which rented me its famous hall but which sullenly opposed a proper announcement of the concert, the insubordination of the orchestra, the demands of the singers for more pay — they imagined that Liszt would pay the expenses — and, finally, complete — and expected failure. My only object was to lay a foundation for the future, nothing more. In spite of everything I managed to get a creditable performance of the Dante symphony and I had the pleasure of hearing it for the first time.

The first part (the Inferno) is wonderfully impressive with its *Francesca da Rimini* interlude, in which burn all the fires of Italian passion. The second part (Purgatory and Paradise) combines the most intense and poignant charm. It contains a fugue episode of unsurpassed beauty.

Ce qu'on entend sur la montagne is, perhaps, the best of the famous symphonic poems. The author was inspired by Victor Hugo's poetry and reproduced its spirit admirably. When will this typical work appear in the concert repertoires? When will orchestra conductors get tired of presenting the three or four Wagnerian works they repeat *ad nauseum*, when they can be heard at the Opéra under better conditions, and Schubert's insignificant *Unfinished Symphony*.

The *Christus* oratorio was given at the first concert of the festival at Heidelberg. It lasted three hours and a half and is so long that I would not dare to advise concert managers to try such an adventure. The performance was sublime. It was given in a newly constructed square hall. Cavaillé-Coll, who knew acoustics, used to advise the square hall for concerts but nobody would listen to him. Three hundred chorus singers, many from a distance, were supported by an orchestra that was large, but, in my opinion, insufficient to stand up against this mass of voices. Furthermore, the orchestra was placed below the level of the stage, as in a theatre, while the voices sounded freely above. Two harps, one on the east side of the stage and one on the west, saw each other from afar,—a pleasingly decorative device, but as annoying to the ear as pleasing to the eye. The chorus and the four soloists—their task was exceedingly arduous—triumphed completely over the difficulties of this immense work and all the varied and delicate nuances were rendered to perfection.

Liszt was far from professing the disdain for the limitations of the human voice that Wagner and Berlioz did. On the contrary he treated it as if it were a queen or a goddess, and it is to be regretted that his tastes did not lead him to work for the stage. Parts of *Saint Elisabeth* show that he would have succeeded and the fashion of having operas for the orchestra, accompanied by voices, which we enjoy today, might have been avoided. He discovered a method, peculiarly his own, of writing choruses. His manner has never been imitated, but it is ingenious and has many advantages. The only trouble about it is that the singers have to take care of details and shadings which is too often the least of their worries. The German societies, where the members sing for pleasure, and not for a salary, are careful to excess, if there can be excess in such matters, and it is their great good fortune to be the interpreters of choruses written in this manner.

It is impossible to give an analysis of this vast work here. We have already spoken of the charming interlude, *Les Bergers à la Crèche*. This pastoral is followed by *Marche des Rois Mages*, a pretty piece, but a little overdeveloped for its intrinsic worth. The vocal parts, *Béatitudes* and *Le Pater Noster*, would be more suitable in a church than in a concert hall. Then come some most brilliant pages,

La Tempête sur le lac de Thibériade, and *Le Mont des Oliviers*, with its baritone solo, and finally, the *Stabat Mater*, where great beauties are combined with terrible length. But nothing in the whole work impressed me more than Christ's entrance to Jerusalem (orchestra, chorus, and soloist) for the reading alone gives no idea of it. Here the author reached the heights. That also describes the delightful effect of the children's chorus singing in the distance *O Filii et Filiae*, harmonised with perfect taste.

While I listened to this beautiful work, I could not help thinking of the great oratorios which crowned Gounod's musical career so gloriously. Liszt and Gounod differed entirely in their musical temperaments, yet in their oratorios they met on common ground. In both there was the same drawing away from the old forms of oratorio, the same search for realism in the expression of the text in music, the same respect for Latin prosody, and the same belief in simplicity of style. But while there is renunciation in the simplicity of Liszt, who threw aside worldly finery to wear the frock of a penitent, on the contrary Gounod appears to return to his original bent with an almost holy joy. This is easily explained. Liszt finished his life in a cassock, while Gounod began his in one. So, despite Liszt's superior refinement, and putting aside exceptional achievements, in this branch of art Gounod was the victor. As there is an *odor di femina* there is a *parfum d'église*, well known to Catholics. Gounod's oratorios are impregnated with this, while it is found in *Christus* very, very feebly, if at all. The *Missa Solemnis* must be examined to find it to any extent in Liszt's work.

All the necessary elements were combined at Heidelberg to produce a magnificent production of Faust and Dante. The orchestra of more than one hundred musicians was perfect. The period when the wind instruments in Germany were wanting both in correctness and quality of sound has passed. But the orchestra conductors have to be taken into account. In our day these gentlemen are *virtuosi*. Their personalities are not subservient to the music, but the music to them. It is the springboard on which they perform and parade their all embracing personalities. They add their own inventions to the author's meaning. Sometimes they draw out the wind instruments so that the musicians have to cut a phrase at the end to catch their breath; again they affect a mad and unrestrained rapidity which allows time neither to play nor to hear the sounds. They hurry or retard the movement for no reason besides their individual caprice or because the author did not indicate them. They perpetrate music of such a disorganized character that the musicians are utterly bewildered, and hesitate in their entrances on account of their inability to distinguish one measure from another.

The delightful *Purgatoire* has become a deadly bore, and the enchanting *Mephistopheles* has been riddled as by a hailstorm. Familiarity with such excesses made me particularly appreciative of the excellent performance that Wolfrum, the musical director, obtained in the vast *Christus* concert.

Among the conductors was Richard Strauss who cannot be passed over without a word. Certainly no one will hope to find moderation and serenity in this artist or be surprised if he gives his temperament free rein, and rides on to victory undisturbed by the ruins he leaves behind. But he lacks neither intelligence nor elegance, and if he sometimes goes too fast he never overemphasizes slowness. When he is conducting, we need not fear the desert of Sahara where others sometimes lead us. Under his direction *Tasso* displayed all its wealth of resources and the jewel-like *Mephisto-Walzer* shone more brightly than ever before.

I can speak but briefly of the numerous soloists. We neither judge nor compare such talents as those of Busoni, Friedheim, and Risler. We are satisfied with admiring them. However, if a prize must be awarded, I should give it to Risler for his masterly interpretation of the great *Sonata in B minor*. He made the most of it in every way, in all its power and in all its delicacy. When it is given in this way, it is one of the finest sonatas imaginable. But such a performance is rare, for it is beyond the average artist. The strength of an athlete, the lightness of a bird, capriciousness, charm, and a perfect understanding of style in general and of the style of this composer in particular are the qualifications needed to perform this work. It is far too difficult for most *virtuosi*, however talented they may be.

Among the women singers I shall only mention Madame Cahier from the Viennese Opera. She is a great artist with a wonderful voice and her interpretation of several *lieder* made them wonderfully worth while. Madame Cahier interpreted the part of Dalila at

Vienna with Dalmores, so it can easily be appreciated how much pleasure I took in hearing her.

A final word about the Dante Symphony. I have read somewhere that Liszt used pages to produce an effect which Berlioz accomplished in the apparition of Mephistopheles in *Faust* with three notes. This comparison is unjust. Berlioz's happy discovery is a work of genius and he alone could have invented it. But the sudden appearance of the Devil is one thing and the depiction of Hell quite another. Berlioz tried such a depiction at the end of the Damnation, and in spite of the strange vocabulary of the chorus, "Irimiru Karabrao, Sat raik Irkimour," and other pretty tricks, he succeeded no better than Liszt. As a matter of fact the opposite was the case.

Chapter XIII

Berlioz's Requiem

The reading of the score of Berlioz's *Requiem* makes it appear singularly old-fashioned, but this is true of most of the romantic dramas, which, like the *Requiem*, show up better in actual performance. It is easy to rail at the vehemence of the Romanticists, but it is not so easy to equal the effect of *Hernani, Lucrèce Borgia* and the *Symphonie fantastique* on the public. For with all their faults these works had a marvellous success. The truth is that their vehemence was sincere and not artificial. The Romanticists had faith in their works and there is nothing like faith to produce lasting results.

Reicha and Leuseur were, as we know, Berlioz's instructors. Leuseur was the author of numerous works and wrote a good deal of church music. Some of his religious works were really beautiful, but he had strange obsessions. Berlioz greatly admired his master and could not help showing, especially in his earlier works, traces of this admiration. That is the reason for the syncopated and jerky passages without rhyme or reason and which can only be explained by his unconscious imitation of Leuseur's faults. In imitating a model the resemblances occur in the faults and not in the excellences, for the latter are inimitable. So the excellences of the *Requiem* are not due to Leuseur but to Berlioz. He had already thrown off the trammels of school and shown all the richness of his vigorous originality to which the value of his scores is due.

In his *Memoirs* Berlioz related the tribulations of his *Requiem*. It was ordered by the government, laid aside for a time, and, finally, performed at the Invalides on the occasion of the capture of Constantine (in Algeria) and the funeral services of General Damrémont. He was astonished at the lack of sympathy and even actual hostility that he encountered. It would have been more astonishing if he had experienced anything else.

Hector Berlioz

We must remember that at this time Berton, who sang *Quand on est toujours vertuex, on aime à voir lever l'aurore*, passed for a great man. Beethoven's symphonies were a novelty, in Paris at least, and a scandal. Haydn's symphonies inspired a critic to write, "What a noise, what a noise!" Orchestras were merely collections of thirty or forty musicians.

We can imagine, therefore, the stupefaction and horror when a young man, just out of school, demanded fifty violins, twenty violas, twenty violoncellos, eighteen contrabasses, four flutes, four oboes, four clarinets, eight bassoons, twelve horns, and a chorus of two hundred voices as a minimum. And that is not all. The *Tuba Mirum* necessitates an addition of thirty-eight trumpets and trombones, divided into four orchestras and placed at the four cardinal points of the compass. Besides, there have to be eight pairs of drums, played by ten drummers, four tam-tams, and ten cymbals.

The story of this array of drums is rather interesting. Reicha, Berlioz's first teacher, had the original idea of playing drum taps in chords of three or four beats. In order to try out this effect, he composed a choral piece, *L'Harmonie des Sphères*, which was published in connection with his *Traité d'Harmonie*. But Reicha's genius did not suffice for this task. He was a good musician, but no more than that. His choral piece was insignificant and remained a dead letter. Berlioz took this lost effect and used it in his *Tuba Mirum*.

However, it must be confessed that this effect does not come up to expectations. In a church or a concert hall we hear a confused and terrifying mingling of sounds, and from time to time we note a change in the depth of tone but we are unable to distinguish the pitch of the chords.

I shall never forget the impression this *Tuba Mirum* made on me when I first heard it at St. Eustache under Berlioz's own direction. It amounted to an absolute neglect of the author's directions. The beginning of the work is marked *moderato*, later, as the brass comes in, the movement is quickened and becomes *andante maestro*. Most of the time the *moderato* was interpreted as an *allegro*, and the *andante maestro* as a simple *moderato*. If the terrific fanfare did not become, as some one ventured to call it, a "Setting Out for the Hunt," it might well have been the accompaniment for a sovereign's entrance to his capital. In order to give this fanfare its grandiose character, the author did not take easy refuge in the wailings of a minor key, but he burst into the splendors of a major key. A certain grandeur of movement alone can preserve its gigantesque quality and impression of power.

Granting all his good intentions, in trying to give us a suggestion of the last judgment by his accumulation of brass, drums, cymbals, and tam-tams, Berlioz makes us think of Thor among the giants trying to empty the drinking-horn which was filled from the sea, and only succeeding in lowering it a little. Yet even that was an accomplishment.

Berlioz spoke scornfully of Mozart's *Tuba Mirum* with its single trombone. "One trombone," he exclaimed, "when a hundred would be none too many!" Berlioz wanted to make us really hear the trumpets of the archangels. Mozart with the seven notes of his one trombone suggested the same idea and the suggestion is sufficient.

We must not forget, however, that here we are in the midst of a world of romanticism, in a world of color and picturesqueness, which could not content itself with so little. And we must remember this fact, if we would not be irritated by the oddities of *L'Hostias*, with its deep trombone notes which seem to come from the very depths of Hell. There is no use in trying to find out what these notes mean. Berlioz told us himself that he discovered these notes at a time when they were almost unknown and he wanted to use them. The contrast between these terrifying notes and the wailing of the flutes is especially curious. We find nothing analogous to this anywhere else.

The delightful *Purgatoire*, where the author sees a chorus of souls in Purgatory, is much better. His Purgatory has no punishments nor any griefs save the awaiting, the long and painful awaiting, of eternal happiness. There is a processional in which the fugue and melody alternate in the most felicitous manner. There are sighs and plaints, all haunting in their extreme expressiveness, a great variety beneath an appearance of monotony, and from time to time two wailing notes. These notes are always the same, as the chorus gives them as a plaint, and they are both affecting and artistic. At the end comes a dim ray of light and hope. This is the only one in the work save the Amen at the end, for Faith and Hope should not be looked for here. The supplications sound like prayers which do not expect to be answered. No one would dare to describe this work as profane, but whether it is religious or not is a question. As Boschot has said, what it expresses above all is terror in the presence of annihilation.

When the *Requiem* was played at the Trocadéro, the audience was greatly impressed and filed out slowly. They did not say, "What a masterpiece!" but "What an orchestra leader!" Nowadays people go to see a conductor direct the orchestra just as they go to hear a tenor, and they arrogate to themselves the right to judge the conductors as they do the tenors. But what a fine sport it is! The qualities of an orchestra conductor which the public appreciates are his elegance, his gestures, his precision, and the expressiveness of his mimicry, all of which are more often directed at the audience than at the orchestra. But all these things are of secondary consideration. What makes up an orchestra conductor's worth are the excellence of execution he obtains from the musicians and the perfect interpretation of the author's meaning — which the audience does not understand. If such an important detail as the author's meaning is obscured and slighted, if a work is disfigured by absurd movements and by an expression which is entirely different from what the author wanted, the public may be dazzled and an execrable conductor, provided his poses are good, may fascinate his audience and be praised to the skies.

Formerly the conductor never saluted his audience. The understanding was that the work and not the conductor was applauded. The Italians and Germans changed all that. Lamoureux was the first to introduce this exotic custom in France. The public was a little surprised at first, but they soon got used to it. In Italy the conductor comes on the stage with the artists to salute the audience. There is nothing more laughable than to see him, as the last note of an opera dies away, jump down from his stand and run like mad to reach the stage in time.

The excellence of the work of English choristers has been highly and justly praised. Perhaps it would be fairer not to praise them so unreservedly when we are so severe on our own. Justice often leaves something to be desired. At all events it must be admitted that Berlioz treated the voices in an unfortunate way. Like Beethoven, he made no distinction between a part for a voice and an instrument. While except for a few rare passages it does not fall as low as the atrocities which disfigure the grandiose *Mass in D*, the vocal part of the *Requiem* is awkwardly written. Singers are ill at ease in it, for the timbre and regularity of the voice resent such treatment. The tenor's part is so written that he is to be congratulated on getting through it without any accident, and nothing more can be expected of him.

What a pity it was that Berlioz did not fall in love with an Italian singer instead of an English tragedienne! Cupid might have wrought a miracle. The author of the *Requiem* would have lost none of his good qualities, but he might have gained, what, for the lack of a better phrase, is called the fingering of the voice, the art of handling it intelligently and making it give without an effort the best effect of which it is capable. But Berlioz had a horror even of the Italian language, musical as that is. As he said in his *Memoirs*, this aversion hid from him the true worth of *Don Juan* and *Le Nozze di Figaro*. One wonders whether he knew that his idol, Gluck, wrote music for Italian texts not only in the case of his first works but also in *Orphée* and *Alceste*. And whether he knew that the aria "*O malheureuse Iphigenie*" was an Italian song badly translated into French. Perhaps he was ignorant of all this in his youth for Berlioz was a genius, not a scholar.

The word genius tells the whole story. Berlioz wrote badly. He maltreated voices and sometimes permitted himself the strangest freaks. Nevertheless he is one of the commanding figures of musical art. His great works remind us of the Alps with their forests, glaciers, sunlight, waterfalls and chasms. There are people who do not like the Alps. So much the worse for them.

Chapter XIV

Pauline Viardot

Alfred de Musset covered Maria Malibran's tomb with immortal flowers and he also told us the story of Pauline Garcia's debut. There is also something about it in Théophile Gautier's writings. It is clear from both accounts that her first appearance was an extraordinary occasion. Natures such as hers reveal themselves at once to those who know and do not have to wait to arrive until they are in full bloom. Pauline was very young at the time, and soon afterwards she married M. Viardot, manager of the Théâtre-Italien and one of the finest men of his day. She went abroad to develop her talent, but she returned in 1849 when Meyerbeer named her to create the rôle of Fides in *Le Prophète*.

Her voice was tremendously powerful, prodigious in its range, and it overcame all the difficulties in the art of singing. But this marvellous voice did not please everyone, for it was by no means smooth and velvety. Indeed, it was a little harsh and was likened to the taste of a bitter orange. But it was just the voice for a tragedy or an epic, for it was superhuman rather than human. Light things like Spanish songs and Chopin mazurkas, which she used to transpose so that she could sing them, were completely transformed by that voice and became the playthings of an Amazon or of a giantess. She lent an incomparable grandeur to tragic parts and to the severe dignity of the oratorio.

I never had the pleasure of hearing Madame Malibran, but Rossini told me about her. He preferred her sister. Madame Malibran, he said, had the advantage of beauty. In addition, she died young and left a memory of an artist in full possession of all her powers. She was not the equal of her sister as a musician and could not have survived the decline of her voice as the latter did.

Madame Viardot was not beautiful, indeed, she was far from it. The portrait by Ary Scheffer is the only one which shows this unequalled woman truthfully and gives some idea of her strange and powerful fascination. What made her even more captivating than her talent as a singer was her personality — one of the most amazing

I have ever known. She spoke and wrote fluently Spanish, French, Italian, English and German. She was in touch with all the current literature of these countries and in correspondence with people all over Europe.

She did not remember when she learned music. In the Garcia family music was in the air they breathed. So she protested against the tradition which represented her father as a tyrant who whipped his daughters to make them sing. I have no idea how she learned the secrets of composition, but save for the management of the orchestra she knew them well. She wrote numerous *lieder* on Spanish and German texts and all of these show a faultless diction. But contrary to the custom of most composers who like nothing better than to show their compositions, she concealed hers as though they were indiscretions. It was exceedingly difficult to persuade her to let one hear them, although the least were highly creditable. Once she sang a Spanish popular song, a wild haunting thing, with which Rubinstein fell madly in love. It was several years before she would admit that she wrote it herself.

Mme. Pauline Viardot

She wrote brilliant operettas in collaboration with Tourguenief, but they were never published and were performed only in private. One anecdote will show her versatility as a composer. She was a friend of Chopin and Liszt and her tastes were strongly futuristic. M. Viardot, on the contrary, was a reactionary in music. He even found Beethoven too advanced. One day they had a guest who was also a reactionary. Madame Viardot sang to them a wonderful work with recitative, aria and final allegro, which they praised to the skies. She had written it expressly for the occasion. I have read this work and even the cleverest would have been deceived.

But it must not be thought from this that her compositions were mere imitations. On the contrary they were extremely original. The only explanation why those that were published have remained unknown and why so many were unpublished is that this admirable artist had a horror of publicity. She spent half her life in teaching pupils and the world knew nothing about it.

During the Empire the Viardots used to give in their apartment on Thursday evenings really fine musical festivals which my surviving contemporaries still remember. From the salon in which the famous portrait by Ary Scheffer was hung and which was devoted to ordinary instrumental and vocal music, we went down a short staircase to a gallery filled with valuable paintings, and finally to an exquisite organ, one of Cavaillé-Coll's masterpieces. In this temple dedicated to music we listened to arias from the oratorios of Handel and Mendelssohn. She had sung them in London, but could not get a hearing for them in the concerts in Paris as they were averse to such vast compositions. I had the honor to be her regular accompanist both at the organ and the piano.

But this passionate lover of song was an all-round musician. She played the piano admirably, and when she was among friends she overcame the greatest difficulties. Before her Thursday audiences, however, she limited herself to chamber music, with a special preference for Henri Reber's duets for the piano and the violin. These delicate, artistic works are unknown to the amateurs of to-day. They seem to prefer to the pure juice of the grape in crystal glasses poisonous potions in cups of gold. They must have orgies, sumptuous ceilings, a deadly luxury. They do not understand the poet who sings, "*O rus, quando te aspiciam!*" They do not appreciate the great distinction of simplicity. Reber's muse is not for them.

Madame Viardot was as learned a musician as any one could be and she was among the first subscribers to the complete edition of Sebastian Bach's works. We know what an astounding revelation that work was. Each year brought ten religious cantatas, and each year brought us new surprises in the unexpected variety and impressiveness of the work. We thought we had known Sebastian Bach, but now we learned how really to know him. We found him a writer of unusual versatility and a great poet. His *Wohltemperirte Klavier* had given us only a hint of all this. The beauties of this famous work needed exposition for, in the absence of definite instructions, opinions differed. In the cantatas the meaning of the words serves as an indication and through the analogy between the forms of expression, it is easy to see pretty clearly what the author intended in his *Klavier* pieces.

One fine day the annual volume was found to contain a cantata in several parts written for a contralto solo accompanied by stringed instruments, oboes and an organ obligato. The organ was there and the organist as well. So we assembled the instruments, Stockhausen, the baritone, was made the leader of the little orchestra, and Madame Viardot sang the cantata. I suspect that the author had never heard his work sung in any such manner. I cherish the memory of that day as one of the most precious in my musical career. My mother and M. Viardot were the only listeners to this exceptional exhibition. We did not dare to repeat it before hearers who were not ready for it. What would now be a great success would have fallen flat at that time. And nothing is more irritating than to see an audience cold before a beautiful work. It is far better to keep to one's self treasures which will be unappreciated.

One thing will always stand in the way of the vogue of Sebastian Bach's vocal works—the difficulty of translation. When they are rendered into French, they lose all their charm and oftentimes become ridiculous.

One of the most amazing characteristics of Madame Viardot's talent was her astonishing facility in assimilating all styles of music. She was trained in the old Italian music and she revealed its beauties as no one else has ever done. As for myself, I saw only its faults. Then she sang Schumann and Gluck and even Glinka whom she sang in Russian. Nothing was foreign to her; she was at home everywhere.

She was a great friend of Chopin and she remembered his playing almost exactly and could give the most valuable directions about the way he interpreted his works. I learned from her that the great pianist's (great musician's, rather) execution was much simpler than has been generally supposed. It was as far removed from any manifestation of bad taste as it was from cold correctness. She told me the secret of the true *tempo rubato* without which Chopin's music is disfigured. It in no way resembles the dislocations by which it is so often caricatured.

I have spoken of her great talent as a pianist. We saw this one evening at a concert given by Madame Schumann. After Madame Viardot had sung some of Schumann's *lieder* with the great pianist playing the accompaniments, the two great artists played the illustrious author's duet for two pianos, which fairly bristles with difficulties, *with equal virtuosity.*

When Madame Viardot's voice began to break, she was advised to devote herself to the piano. If she had, she would have found a new career and a second reputation. But she did not want to make the change, and for several years she presented the sorry spectacle of genius contending with adversity. Her voice was broken, stubborn, uneven, and intermittent. An entire generation knew her only in a guise unworthy of her.

Her immoderate love of music was the cause of the early modification of her voice. She wanted to sing everything she liked and she sang Valentine in *Les Huguenots,* Donna Anna in *Don Juan,* besides other rôles she should never have undertaken if she wanted to preserve her voice. She came to realize this at the end of her life. "Don't do as I did," she once told a pupil. "I wanted to sing everything, and I ruined my voice."

Happy are the fiery natures which burn themselves out and glory in the sword that wears away the scabbard.

Chapter XV

Orphée

We know, or, rather we used to know—for we are beginning to forget that there is an admirable edition of Gluck's principal works. This edition was due to the interest of an unusual woman, Mlle. Fanny Pelletan, who devoted a part of her fortune to this real monument and to fulfill a wish Berlioz expressed in one of his works. Mlle. Pelletan was an unusually intelligent woman and an accomplished musician, but she needed some one to help her in this large and formidable task. She was unassuming and distrusted her own powers, so that she secured as a collaborator a German musician, named Damcke, who had lived in Paris a long time and who was highly esteemed. He gave her the moral support she needed and some bad advice as well, which she felt obliged to follow. This collaboration accounts for the change of the contralto parts to counter-tenors. It also accounts for the fact that in every instance the parts for the clarinets are indicated in C, in this way attributing to the author a formal intention he never had. Gluck wrote the parts for the clarinets without bothering whether the player—to whom he left a freedom of choice and the work of transposition—would use his instrument in C, B, or A. This method was not peculiar to Gluck. Other composers used it as well, and traces of it are found even in Auber's works.

After Damcke's death Mlle. Pelletan got me to help her in this work. I wanted to change the method, but the edition would have lost its unity and she would not consent. It was time that Damcke's collaboration ended. He belonged to the tribe of German professors who have since become legion. Due to their baneful influence, in a short time, when the old editions have disappeared, the works of Haydn, Mozart, and Beethoven, even of Chopin, will be all but unrecognizable. The works of Sebastian Bach and Handel will be the only ones in existence in their pristine purity of form, thanks to the admirable editions of the *Bach und Händel Gesselschaft*. When Mlle. Pelletan brought me into the work, the two *Iphigenie* had been published; *Alceste* was about to be, and *Armide* was ready. In *Armide* Damcke had been entirely carried away by his zeal for "improvements"—a zeal that can do so much harm. It was time this was stopped. Not only had he corrected imaginary faults here and there, but he had also inserted things of his own invention. He had even gone so far as to re-orchestrate the ballet music, in the naïve belief that he was bringing out the author's real meaning better than he had done himself. It took an enormous amount of time to undo this mischief, for I distrusted somewhat my own lights and Mlle. Pelletan had too high an opinion of Damcke's work and did not dare to override his judgment.

That excellent woman did not live to see the end of her work. She began the preparation of Orphée, but she died almost at once. So I was left to finish the score alone without that valuable experience and masterly insight by which she solved the most difficult problems. And there were real enigmas to be solved at every step. The old engraved scores of Gluck's works reproduced his manuscripts faithfully enough, but they bore evidence of carelessness and amazing inaccuracy. They are mere sketches instead of complete scores. Many details are vague and vagueness is not permissible in a serious edition. It follows that the different editions of Gluck's works published in the Nineteenth Century, however sumptuous or careful they may be, are worthless. The Pelletan edition alone can be consulted with confidence, because we were the only ones to have all extant and authentic documents in the library at the Opéra to set us right. We had scores copied for actual performances on the stage and portions of orchestral parts of incalculable value. In addition, we had no aim or preoccupation in elaborating this material other than to reconstitute as closely as possible the thought of the author.

Switzerland is a country where artistic productions are not unusual. Every year we have reports of some grandiose performance in which the people take part themselves. They come from every direction to help, even from a considerable distance, thanks to the many means of communication in that delightful land. It is not surprising, therefore, to learn that a theatre has been built in the pretty town of Mézières, near Lusanne, for the performance of the works of a young poet, named Morax. These works are dramas with choruses, and the surrounding country furnishes the singers. The work given in 1911 was Allenor—the music by Gustave Doret—and it was a great success.

Gustave Doret is a real artist and he never for a moment thought of keeping the Théâtre du Jorat for his own exclusive use. He dreamt of giving Gluck's works in their original form, for they are always altered and changed according to the fancies or incompetency of the performers or directors. They formed a large and influential committee and a substantial guarantee fund was subscribed. Then they gave a brilliant banquet at which the Princess of Brancovan was present. And Paderewski, one of the most enthusiastic promotors of the enterprise, delivered an eloquent address. No one should be surprised at either his zeal or his eloquence. Paderewski is not only a pianist; he is a man of great intellect as well,—a great artist who permits himself the luxury of playing the piano marvellously.

As he knew that I had spent several years in studying Gluck's works under the microscope, so to speak, Gustave Doret did me the honor to ask my advice. His choice for the opening work was *Orphée*, which requires only three principals, Orpheus, Eurydice, and Love. It has become the custom to add a fourth, a Happy Spirit, but this spirit is one of Carvalho's inventions and has no reason for existence.

There are, however, two *Orphée*. The first is *Orfeo* which was written in Italian, on Calzabigi's text, and was first presented at Venice in 1761. The rôle of Orpheus in this score was written for a contralto and was designed for the eunuch Quadagni. The Venetian engravers of that day were either incompetent or, perhaps, there were none, for the scores of Gluck's *Alceste* in Italian and Haydn's *Seasons* were printed from type. However that may be the score of *Orfeo* was engraved in Paris. The composer Philidor corrected the proofs. He little thought that *Orfeo* would ever get so far as Paris, so he appropriated the romanza in the first act and introduced it with but slight modifications into his opéra-comique *Le Sorcier*. Later on Marie Antoinette called Gluck to Paris and thus afforded him the opportunity for the complete development of his genius. After he had written *Iphigenie en Aulide*, performed in 1774, especially for the Opéra, he had the idea of adapting *Orfeo* for the French stage. To tell the truth he must have thought of it before, for *Orphée* appeared at the Opéra only three months after *Iphigenie* and it had been entirely rewritten in collaboration with Moline. The contralto part had been changed to tenor and so the principal rôle was given to Legros.

While it may be true that the author improved this work in the French version, it is not true in every case. There is some question whether the overture existed in the Italian score. It is generally believed that it did, but there are old copies of this version in existence and they begin the opera with the funeral chorus and show no overture at all. This overture, although the *Mercure de France* treats it as a "beautiful symphonic piece which serves as a good introduction to the work," in reality does not resemble the style of the rest at all. It in no way prepares for that admirable chorus at the beginning — unequaled of its kind — which Orpheus's broken hearted cry of "Eurydice! Eurydice!" makes so pathetic.

The first act of *Orfeo* ends in a tumultuous effect of the stringed instruments which was evidently intended to indicate a change of scene and the appearance of the stage settings of the infernal regions. This passage does not appear in the French *Orphée* and it is lacking in the engraved score, where it is replaced by a bravura aria of doubtful taste, accompanied by a single quartet. Whether the stage managers wanted an entr'acte or the tenor, Legros, demanded an effective aria, or for both these reasons, a reading of the manuscript indicates how absolutely the author's meaning was changed. There is no doubt that except for some such reason he would have changed this aria and put it in harmony with the rest of the work.

For a long time this aria was attributed to Bertoni, the composer, and Gluck was accused of plagiarizing it. As a matter of fact, and to the contrary, this aria came from an older Italian opera of Gluck's. Bertoni not only imitated it in one of his scores, but he had the hardihood to write an *Orfeo* on the text already followed by Gluck in which he plagiarized the work of his illustrious predecessor in a scandalous fashion.

This same aria, changed with real genius and performed with prodigious eclat by Madame Viardot, and re-orchestrated by myself, was one of the strongest reasons for the success of the famous performances at the Théâtre-Lyrique. But it is well understood that it could not properly find a place in an edition where the sole end was artistic sincerity and purity of the text.

From this point of view it would seem that the best manner of giving *Orphée* would be to conform to the author's definitive version. A tenor would have to take the part of Orpheus, since we no longer have male contraltos, and to keep to this kind of a voice in *Orphée* we would have to have recourse to what is called, in theatrical terms, a *travesti*. There are obstacles to this, however. The pitch has changed since the Eighteenth Century; it has gone up and it is now impossible, or nearly so, to sing the rôle written for Legros. The contraltos of the Italian chorus have become the counter-tenors, who, for the same reason, find themselves struggling with too sharp notes.

In the Seventeenth Century the French pitch was even more flat, and it is a great pity, for it is almost impossible to perform our old music, on account of the insuperable obstacles. This is not the case in Germany, however, or in Italy, and that is the reason why the works of Sebastian Bach and Mozart can be sung. The same is true of Gluck's Italian works.

This was the reason that Doret gave the part of Orpheus to a contralto, just as is done at the Opéra-Comique. The poetic character of the part of Orpheus lends itself excellently to such a feminine interpretation. But in resuming the key of the Italian score, it is necessary to go back, at least to a considerable degree, to the instrumentation. By a curious anomaly the beautiful recitative, accompanied by the murmur of brooks and the songs of the birds, is in C major in both scores. The author could not have changed them. On the contrary he modified his instrumentation greatly, simplified and perfected it.

We know that the authors, in utter defiance of mythology, wanted a happy ending and so brought Eurydice back to life a second time. Love accomplished this miracle and the work ended with the song "Love Triumphs," which is exceedingly joyful and in harmony with the situation. They did not want this ending, which was in *Orfeo* and which Gluck retained in *Orphée*, at the old Théâtre-Lyrique and the Opéra-Comique, and they replaced it with a chorus by Echo and Narcissus. This chorus is charming, but that does not excuse it. Joy was what the author wanted and this does not give joy at all. Gluck's finale is regarded as not sufficiently distinguished, but this is wrong. The real finale was sung at Mézières and it was found that it was not at all common, but that its frank gaiety was in the best of taste.

Gluck had no scruples about grinding several grists from the same sack and drawing from his old works to help out his new ones. So the parasitical aria attributed to Bertoni was written by Gluck in the first place in 1764 for a soprano. He wove this into his opera *Aristo* in 1769. This is also true of the trio, *Tendre Amour*, which precedes the finale in the last act. A serious-minded analyst might be tempted to admire the profound psychology of the author in mingling doleful accents with expressions of joy, but he would have his labor for his pains. The trio was taken from the opera *Elena e Paride*, where Gluck expressed strongly wrought up emotions. Doret did not keep these two passages and one can't blame him. On the other hand, he retained, by making it an entr'acte, the *Ballet des Furies*. This was taken from a ballet, *Don Giovanni o il convitato de pietra*, which was performed at Vienna in 1761. This passage was used as the accompaniment to Don Juan's descent into Hell, surrounded by his band of demons.

Many of Gluck's compatriots came to Mézières to see *Orphée* and they were loyal enough to recognize the superiority of the performance. Some even had the courage to say, "We murder Gluck in Germany."

I discovered that fact a long time ago. In my youth I was indignant when I saw Paris, where Gluck wrote his finest works, quite neglecting them, whereas Germany continued to promote them. In those days I was frequently called to the other side of the Rhine to play in concerts, and I watched for a chance to see one of these masterpieces which had been forgotten in France. So it was with the liveliest joy that one day I entered one of the leading German theaters where they were giving *Armide*. What a hollow mockery it was!

Madame Malten was Armide, and she was everything that could be wished in voice, talent, style, beauty and charm. She spoke French without an accent and was as remarkable as an actress as a singer, so she would without doubt have had great success at the Opéra in Paris. She was Armide herself, an irresistible enchantress.

But the rest! Renaud was a raw boy, and his shaven chin brought out in sharp relief enormous black moustaches with long waxed ends. He had a voice, to be sure, but no style, and no understanding of the work he was trying to interpret.

Hidradot is an old sorcerer tempered in the fires of Hell. He enters, saying:

> "I see hard by Death that threatens me,
>
> And already old age, that has chilled my blood,
>
> Is on me, bowing me beneath a crushing burden."

Imagine my surprise at seeing come on the stage a magnificent specimen of manhood, with a curled black beard, in all the glory of his youth and vigor superbly arrayed in a red cloak trimmed with gold!

The stage setting was also extraordinary. In the second act Renaud went to sleep at the back of the stage, forcing Armide to speak the whole of the beautiful scene which follows, one of the most important in the part, at a distance from the footlights and with her back to the audience.

As for the orchestra, sometimes it followed Gluck's text and sometimes it borrowed bits of orchestration which Meyerbeer had written for the Opéra at Berlin. This orchestration is interesting, and I know it well for I have had it in hand. It is only fair to say that Gluck, from some inexplicable caprice, did not give the same care to the instrumentation of *Armide* that he did to *Orphée*, *Alcesti*, and the *Iphigenies*. The trombones do not appear at all and the drums and flutes only at rare intervals. Re-orchestration is not absolutely necessary and Meyerbeer's is no more reprehensible than those with which Mozart enriched Handel's *Messe* and *La Fête d'Alexandre*. What was inadmissible was not deciding frankly for one version or the other. It was like a badly patched coat which shows the old cloth in one place and the new in another.

Afterwards I saw *Armide* treated in another way.

Did you ever happen to cherish the memory of a delightful and picturesque city, where everything made a harmonious whole, where the beautiful walks were arched over by old trees—and later come back to it to find it embellished, the trees cut down, the walks replaced by enormous buildings which dwarfed into insignificance the ancient marvels which gave the city its charm?

This was the case with me when I saw *Armide* again in a city which I shall not name. The opera had been judged superannuated and had been "improved." A young composer had written a new score in which he inserted here and there such bits of Gluck as he thought worthy of being preserved. A costly and magnificently imbecile luxuriousness set off the whole piece. I may be pardoned the cruel adjective when I say that in the scene of Hate, so deeply inspired, and which takes place in a sort of cave, they relegated the chorus to the wings to make a place for dragons, fantastic birds beating their wings, and other deviltries. This, of course, deprived the chorus of all its power and distinction.

But the best was at the end of the second act. The forest with its trees, grass and rocks entirely disappeared in the flies taking Renaud and Armide with it and the spectator was left, for some unknown reason, looking at a background surrounded by mountains. Then, by a marvel of mechanism, there appeared to the sound of ultramodern music, Renaud sleeping on a bed of state, with Armide standing at the foot and stretching forth her hand with a gesture of authority, declaiming in a solemn tone,

"Rinaldo, I love you!"

and the curtain fell to the applause of the audience.

We owe much to Germany in music, for it has produced many great musicians. It can set off against our trinity of Corneille, Racine, and Molière, the no less glorious Haydn, Mozart and Beethoven. But Germany seems to have lost all respect for the meaning of its own music and for its own glories. Instead of watching over the purity of the text of its masterpieces, it alters them at its pleasure and makes them all but unrecognizable. We abuse nuances but they were rare in earlier days. An orchestra conductor who performs symphonies by Haydn and Mozart, even by Beethoven, has the right to make additions. But it is intolerable that the scores should be printed with these nuances and bowings which are in no way due to the author and which are imposed by the editor. Nevertheless, that is what happens, and it is impossible to tell where the authentic text ends and the interpolation begins. In addition, the interpolation may be the exact contrary of what the author intended.

This evil is at its worst in piano music. Our famous teachers, like Marmontel and Le Couppey, have published editions of the classics which are full of their own directions. But the player is forewarned; it is the Marmontel or Le Couppey edition and makes no pretence of authenticity. In Germany, however, there are supposedly authentic editions, based on the originals, but which superimpose their own pernicious inventions on the author's text.

The touch of the piano used to be different from what it is to-day. The directions in Mozart's and Beethoven's works show that they used the execution of stringed instruments as their model. The touch was lighter and the fingers were raised so that the notes were separated slightly, and not run together except when indicated. The supposition is that this must have led to a dryness of tone. I remember to have heard in my childhood some old people whose playing was singularly hopping. Then, there came a reaction, and with it a passion for slurring the notes. When I was Stamaty's pupil, it was considered most difficult to "tie" the notes; that required, however, only dexterity and suppleness. "When she learns to 'tie,' she will know how to play," said the mother of a young pianist. Nevertheless, the trick of perpetual *legato* becomes exceedingly monotonous and takes away all character from the pianoforte classics. But it is insisted on everywhere in the modern German editions. Throughout there are connections seemingly interminable in length, and indications of *legato, sempre legato*, which the author not only did not indicate, but in places where it is easy to see that he intended the exact opposite.

If this is the case, what shall be said of marking the fingering on all the notes—which often makes good playing impossible. Liszt taught hundreds of pupils according to the best principles, yet such erroneous principles have prevailed!

Disciples of the ivory keys are numerous in our day. Everybody wants to have a piano, and everybody plays it or thinks he does, which is not always the same thing, and few really understand what the term "to play the piano," so currently used, means.

The harpsichord reigned supreme before the appearance of the piano—an instrument which is beloved by some and execrated by others. To his utter amazement Reyer was considered an enemy of the pianoforte. The harpsichord has been revived of late so that it is needless to describe it. It lacks strength, and that was the reason it was dethroned in a period when strength was everything. On the other hand, it has distinction and elegance. As the player can not modify the intensity of the sound by a single pressure of the finger—in which it resembles the organ—like the organ, with its multiple keyboards and registers, the harpsichord has a wide variety of effects and affords the opportunity for several octaves to sound simultaneously. As a result, while music written for the harpsichord gains in strength and expression on the modern instrument, it often assumes a deceptive monotony for which the author is not responsible.

The players of the harpsichord were ignorant of muscular effects; there was nothing of the unchained lion about them. The delicate hands of a marquise lost none of their gracefulness as they skimmed over the keyboards, and the red or black keys emphasized their whiteness.

The introduction of the hammer in the place of the tiny nib permitted the modification of the quality of sound by differences in the pressure of the fingers, and also the production at will of such nuances as *forte* and *piano* without recourse to the different registers. This is the reason why the new instrument was first called the pianoforte. The word was long and cumbersome and was cut in half. When it became necessary to *assault* the note, they used the phrase "to hit the forte." The papers which gave accounts of young Mozart's concerts praised him for his ability to "hit."

Nevertheless one did not hit hard. These keyboards with their limited keys responded so easily that a child's fingers were sufficient. I first played on one of these instruments at the age of three. It was made by Zimmerman, whose son was Gounod's father-in-law.

Later, the weight of the keys was increased to get a greater volume of sound. Then, when long-haired *virtuosi*, playing by main strength, produced peals of thunder, they really "*toucha du piano.*"

To return to *Orphée* and end as we began, I have to make a painful confession. If the works of Gluck in general and *Orphée* in particular have had a happy influence on our musical taste, a passage from this last work has been a noxious influence, — the famous chorus of the demons "*Quel est l'audacieux – qui dans ces sombres lieux – ose porter ses pas?*"

In the old days French opera was based on declamation and it was scrupulously respected even in the arias. There is a fine example of this excellent system in Lully's famous aria from *Medusa* to prove what strength results from a close relation between the accent of the verse and the music. Gluck was one of the most fervent disciples of this system, but *Orphée*, as we know, was derived from *Orfeo*. The question was whether he could even think of suppressing this spectacular chorus with its amazing strength which was one of the principal reasons for the work's success. Unfortunately the music of the chorus was moulded on the Italian text, and each verse ended with the accent on the antepenult, which occurs frequently in German and Italian, but never in French. And they sing:

Quel est l'au*dac*ieux

Qui dans ces *som*bres lieux

Ose por*ter* ses pas

Et devant *le* trepas

Ne frémit pas?

As French is not strongly accented such faults are tolerated. Gluck's theme impressed itself on the memory, so that he dealt a terrific blow to the purity of prosody. We gradually became so disinterested in this that by Auber's time scarcely any attention was paid to it. Finally, Offenbach appeared. He was a German by birth and his musical ideas naturally rhymed with German in direct contradiction to the French words to which they applied. This constant bungling passed for originality. Sometimes it would have been necessary to change the division of a measure to get a correct melody, as in the song:

Un p'tit bonhomme

Pas plus haut qu'ça.

In such a case we might say that he did wrong for the mere pleasure of going astray. But popular taste was so corrupted that no one noticed it and everybody who wrote in the lighter vein fell into the same habits.

We owe a debt of gratitude to André Messager for breaking away from this manner and setting musical phraseology aright. His return to the old traditions was not the least of the attractions of his delightful *Véronique*.

But we are wandering far from Gluck and *Orphée*, although not so far as we might think. In art, as in everything, extremes meet, and there are all kinds of tastes.

Chapter XVI

Delsarte

Felix Duquesnal in one of his brilliant articles has written something about Delsarte, the singer, in connection with his controversy with Madame Carvalho. The cause of this controversy was the lessons she took from him. The name of Delsarte should never be forgotten, as I shall try to explain. Madame Carvalho did not refuse to pay Delsarte for her lessons, but she did not want to be called his pupil. Although she had attended the Conservatoire, she wanted to be known solely as a pupil of Duprez. As a matter of fact it was Duprez who knew how to make the "Little Miolan," the delightful warbler, into the great singer with her important place on the French stage.

But this was accomplished at a price. Madame Carvalho told me about it herself. Her medium register was weak and Duprez undertook to substitute chest tones and develop clearness as much as possible. "When I began to work," she said, "my mother was frightened. One would have thought that a calf was being killed in the house."

Ordinarily such a method would produce a harsh, shaky voice and all freshness would be lost. But in Madame Carvalho's case the opposite was true. The freshness and purity of her voice were beyond compare, while its smoothness and the harmony of the registers were perfect. It was a miracle the like of which we shall probably never see again.

But if Duprez made a wonderful voice at the risk of breaking it, I have always thought that Madame Carvalho owed her admirable diction, so distinguishing a mark of her talent, to Delsarte. Delsarte was a disastrous and deadly teacher of singing. No voice could stand up under his methods, not even his own, although he attributed its loss to teaching at the Conservatoire. But he studied deeply the arts of speaking and gesture, and he was a past master in them.

I once attended a course he gave in these subjects. He stated highly illuminating truths and gave the psychological reasons for accents and the physiological reasons for the gestures. He determined the use of gestures in some sort of scientific way. Mystic fancies were mixed up in these questions.

It was extremely interesting to see him dissect one of Fontaine's fables or a passage from Racine, and to hear him explain why the accent should be on such a word or on such a syllable and not on another, to bring out the sense. Although this course was so instructive, few took it, for Delsarte was almost unknown to people. His influence scarcely extended outside a narrow circle of admirers, but the quality made up for the quantity. This was the circle of the old *Debats*, which was formerly devoted exclusively to Romanticism, but at this time to the classics—the set headed by Ingres in painting and Reber in music. Theirs was a secluded and ascetic world in silent revolt against the abominations of the century. One had to hear the tone of devotion in which the members of this circle spoke of the ancients to appreciate their attitude. Nothing in our day can give any idea of them. "They say," one of the devotees once told me, "that the ancients learned Beauty through a sort of revelation, and Beauty has steadily degenerated ever since."

Such false notions were, however, professed by the most sincere people who were deeply devoted to art. So this group, which had no influence on their own contemporaries, nevertheless, without knowing it or wishing to do so, played a useful rôle.

As we know, the public was divided into two camps. On one side were the partisans of Melody, opéra-comique, the Italians, and, with some effort, of grand opera. Opposed to them were the partisans of music in the grand style—Beethoven, Mozart, Haydn, and Sebastian Bach, although he was little known and is less well known now.

No one gave a thought to our old French school, to the composers from Lulli to Gluck, who produced so many excellent works. Reber showed Delsarte the way and the latter, naturally an antiquarian, threw himself into this unexplored field with surprising vigor. Only Lulli's name was known, while Campra, Mondonville and the others were entirely forgotten. Even Gluck himself had been forgotten. First editions of his orchestral scores, which it is impossible to find to-day, sold for a few francs at the second-hand book shops. Rameau was never mentioned.

Delsarte, handsome, eloquent, and fascinating, wielded an almost imperial sway over his little coterie of artists. Thanks to him the lamp of our old French school was kept dimly burning until the day when inherent justice permitted it to be revived. In this restricted world no evening was complete without Delsarte. He would come in with some story of frightful throat trouble to justify his chronic lack of voice, and, then, without any voice at all but by a kind of magic, would put shudders into the tones of Orpheus or Eurydice. I often played his accompaniments and he always demanded *pianissimo*.

"But," I would say, "the author has indicated *forte*."

"That is true," he would answer, "but in those days the harpsichord had little depth of tone."

It would have been easy to answer that the accompaniment was written for the orchestra and not for the harpsichord.

Delsarte's execution, on account of the insufficiency of his vocal powers, was often entirely different from what the author intended. Furthermore, he was absolutely ignorant of the correct way to interpret the appogiatures and other marks which are not used today. As a result his interpretation of the older works was inexact. But that did not matter, for even if masterpieces are presented badly, there is always something left. Besides, both the singer and his hearers had Faith. He had a way of pronouncing "Gluck" which aroused expectation even before one heard a note.

From time to time Delsarte gave a concert. He would come on the stage and say that he had a bad throat, but that he would try to give *Iphigenia's Dream* or something of that sort. His courage would prove to be greater than his strength and he would have to stop. He would then fall back on old-time songs or La Fontaine's fables in which he excelled. A skilfully studied mimicry, which seemed entirely natural, underlay his reading. A red handkerchief, which he knew how to draw from his pocket at just the proper moment, always excited applause.

One day he conceived the idea of giving one of Bossuet's sermons at his concert. Religious authority was very powerful at the time and forbade it. Yet there would have been no sacrilege, and I regretted keenly that I could not hear this magnificent prose delivered so wonderfully. Now that religious authority has lost its secular support, we see things in an entirely different way. Christ, the Virgin, and the Saints walk the stage, speak in prose or verse, and sing. It would seem that no one is shocked for there is no protest. For my own part I must frankly confess that such pseudo-religious exhibitions are disagreeable. They disturb me greatly and I can see no use in them.

In order to foster admiration for the old masters, Delsarte conceived the idea of publishing a collection of pieces taken from their works right and left, and, as a result, he created his *Archives du Chant*. He had special type made and the publication was a marvel of beautiful typography, correctness and good taste. At the beginning of each part was a cleverly harmonised passage of church music. The support of a publisher was necessary for the success of such a work, but Delsarte was his own publisher and he met with no success at all. Similar but inferior publications have been markedly successful.

Delsarte aimed at purity of text, but his successors have been forced to modernize the works to make them accessible for the public. This fact is painful. In literature the texts are studied and the endeavor is to reproduce the writer's thought as closely as possible. In music it is entirely different. With each new edition a professor is commissioned to supervise the work and he adds something of his own invention.

Delsarte, a singer without a voice, an imperfect musician, a doubtful scholar, guided by an intuition which approached genius, in spite of his numerous faults played an important rôle in the evolution of French music in the Nineteenth Century. He was no ordinary man. The impression he gave to all who knew him was of a visionary, an apostle. When one heard him speak with his fiery enthusiasm about these works of the past which the world had forgotten, one could but believe that such oblivion was unjust and desire to know these relics of another age.

Without the shadow of a doubt I owed to his leadership the necessary courage to make a profound study of the works of the old school, for they are unattractive at first. Berlioz berated all this music. He had seen Gluck's works on the stage in his youth, but he could see nothing in them that was not "superannuated and childish." With all respect to Berlioz's memory, it deserved a kinder judgment than that. When one reaches the depths of this music, although it may be at the price of some effort, he is well repaid for his pains. There is real feeling, grandeur and even something of the picturesque in these works — as much as could be with the means at their disposal.

It is only right that we should pay tribute to Delsarte's memory. He was a pioneer who, during his whole life, proclaimed the value of immortal works, which the world despised. That is no slight merit.

Chapter XVII

Seghers

While Delsarte was preparing the way for the old French opera and above all for Gluck's works, another pioneer of musical evolution was working to form the taste of the Parisian public, but with an entirely different power and another effect. Seghers was the man. He played a great rôle and his memory should be honored.

As his name indicates, Seghers was a Belgian. He started life as a violinist and was one of Baillot's pupils. His execution was masterly, his tone admirable, and he had a musical intelligence of the first order. He had every right to a first rank among *virtuosi*, but this man, herculean in appearance and tenacious in his purposes, lost all his power before an audience.

He had a dream of giving to lovers of music the last of Beethoven's quartets, which were considered at the time both unplayable and incomprehensible. In the end he planned a series of concerts at which, despite my age—I was only fifteen—I was to be the regular pianist. He planned to give in addition to these quartets, some of Bach's sonatas and Reber's and Schumann's trios. I spoke of this plan to his mother-in-law one day as she was peacefully embroidering at the window, and told her how pleased I was at the thought of the concerts.

"Don't count on it too much," she told me. "He'll never give them."

When everything was ready, he invited some thirty people to listen to a trial performance. It was wretched. All the depth of tone had gone from his violin as well as the skill from his fingers.... The project was abandoned.

It was left for Maurin to make something out of these terrible quartets. Maurin had peculiar gifts. He had a lightness of bow which I have never seen equalled by anyone and a lightness and charm which enchanted the public. But I can say in all sincerity that Seghers's execution was even better. Unfortunately for him I was his only listener.

Madame Seghers was a woman of great beauty, unusually intelligent and distinguished. She had been one of Liszt's pupils and was a pianist of first rank. But she was even more timid than her husband—a single listener was sufficient to paralyze her. When Liszt was teaching Madame Seghers, he came to appreciate her husband's real worth and entrusted his daughter's musical education to him. This is sufficient indication of the esteem in which Liszt held Seghers. So it was not surprising that he gave me valuable and greatly needed suggestions in regard to style and the piano itself, for his friendship with Liszt had given him a thorough understanding of the instrument.

I first saw and heard Liszt at Seghers's house. He had reappeared in Paris after long years of absence, and by that time he had begun to seem almost legendary. The story went that since he had become chapel-master at Weimar he was devoting himself to grand compositions, and, what appeared unbelievable, "piano music." People who ought to have known that Mozart was the greatest pianist of his time shrugged their shoulders at this. As a climax it was insinuated that Liszt was setting systems of philosophy to music.

I studied Liszt's works with all the enthusiasm of my eighteen years for I already regarded him as a genius and attributed to him even before I saw him almost superhuman powers as a pianist. Remarkable to relate he surpassed the conception I had formed. The dreams of my youthful imagination were but prose in comparison with the Bacchic hymn evoked by his supernatural fingers. No one who did not hear him at the height of his powers can have any idea of his performance.

Seghers was a member of the Société des Concerts at the Conservatoire. This reached only a restricted public and there was no other symphony concert worthy of the name in Paris at the time. And if the public was limited, the repertoire was even more so. Haydn's, Mozart's and Beethoven's symphonies were played almost exclusively, and Mendelssohn's were introduced with the greatest difficulty. Only fragments of vast compositions like the oratorios were given. An author who was still alive was looked upon as an intruder. However, the conductor was permitted to introduce a solo of his own selection. Thus my friend Auguste Tolbecque, who was over eighty, was permitted to give—he still played beautifully—my first *concerto* for the violoncello which I had written for him. Deldevez, the conductor of the famous orchestra at the time, did not overlook the chance to tell me that he had put my *concerto* on the programme only through consideration for Tolbecque. Otherwise, he added, he would have preferred Messieurs So-and-so's.

Not only did the Conservatoire audiences know little music, but the larger public knew none at all. The symphonies of the three great classic masters were known to amateurs for the most part only through Czerny's arrangement for two pianos.

This was the situation when Seghers left the Société des Concerts and founded the Société St. Cécile. He led the orchestra himself. The new society took its name from the St. Cécile hall which was then in the Rue de la Chaussée d'Antin. It was a large square hall and was excellent in spite of the prejudice in favor of halls with curved lines for music. Curved surfaces, as Cavaillé-Coll, who was an expert in this matter, once told me, distort sound as curved mirrors distort images. Halls used for music should, therefore, have only straight lines. The St. Cécile hall was sufficiently large to allow a complete orchestra and chorus to be placed properly and heard as well.

Seghers managed to assemble an excellent and sizable orchestra and he also secured soloists who were young then but who have since become celebrities. The orchestra was poorly paid and also very unruly. I have seen them rebel at the difficulties in Beethoven, and it was even worse when Seghers undertook to give Schumann who was considered the *ne plus ultra* of modernism. Oftentimes there were real riots. But we heard there for the first time the overture of *Manfred*, Mendelssohn's *Symphony in A minor*, and the overture to *Tannhauser*.

The modern French school found the doors in the Rue Bergère closed to them, but they were welcomed with open arms at the Chaussée d'Antin. Among them were Reber, Gounod, and Gouvy, and even beginners like Georges Bizet and myself. I made my first venture there with my *Symphony in E flat* which I wrote when I was seventeen. In order to get the committee to adopt it, Seghers offered it as a symphony by an unknown author, which had been sent to him from Germany. The committees swallowed the bait, and the symphony, which would probably not had a hearing if my name had been signed, was praised to the skies.

I can still see myself at a rehearsal listening to a conversation between Berlioz and Gounod. Both of them were greatly interested in me, so that they spoke freely and discussed the excellences and faults of this anonymous symphony. They took the work seriously and it can be imagined how I drank in their words. When the veil of mystery was lifted, the interest of the two great musicians changed to friendship. I received a letter from Gounod, which I have kept carefully, and as it does credit to the author, I take the liberty of reproducing it here:

> My dear Camille:
>
> I was officially informed yesterday that you are the author of the symphony which they played on Sunday. I suspected it; but now that I am sure, I want to tell you at once how pleased I was with it. You are beyond your years; always keep on—and remember that on Sunday, December 11, 1853, you obligated yourself to become a great master.
>
> Your pleased and devoted friend,
>
> CH. GOUNOD.

Many works which had been unknown to Parisian audiences were given at these concerts and nowhere else. Among them were Schubert's *Symphony in C,* fragments of Weber's opera *Préciosa*, his *Jubel overture*, and symphonies by Gade, Gouvy, Gounod, and Reber. These symphonies are not dazzling but they are charming. They form an interesting link in the golden chain, and the public has a right and even some sort of duty to hear them. They would enjoy hearing them too, just as at the Louvre they like to see certain pictures which are not extraordinary but which are, nevertheless, worthy of the place they occupy. That is to say, if the public is really guided by a love of art and seeks only intellectual pleasure instead of sensations and shocks. Some one has said lately that where there is no feeling there is no music. We could, however, cite many passages of music which are absolutely lacking in emotion and which are beautiful nevertheless from the standpoint of pure esthetic beauty. But what am I saying? Painting goes its own way and emotion, feeling, and passion are evoked by the least landscape. Maurice Barres brought in this fashion and he could even see passion in rocks. Happy is he who can follow him there.

Among the things we heard at that time and which we never hear now I must note especially Berlioz's *Corsaire* and *King Lear*. His name is so much beloved by the present day public that this neglect is both unjust and unjustifiable. The great man himself came to the Société St. Cécile one day to conduct his *L'Enfance du Christ* which he had just written — or rather *La Fuite en Egypt* which was the only part of the work that was in existence then. He composed the rest of it afterwards. I remember perfectly the performances which the great man directed. They were lively and spirited rather than careful, but somewhat slower than what Edouard Colonne has accustomed us to. The time was faster and the nuances sharper.

In spite of the enthusiasm of the conductor and the skill and talent of the orchestra, the society led a hand-to-mouth existence. The sinews of war were lacking. Weckerlin directed the choruses and I acted as the accompanist at the rehearsals. Love of art sufficed us, but the singers and instrumentalists were not satisfied with that in the absence of all emoluments. If Seghers had been adaptable, he might have secured resources, but that was not his forte. Meyerbeer wanted him to give his *Struensée* and Halévy wanted a performance of his *Prométhée*. But this was contrary to Seghers's convictions, and when he had once made up his mind nothing could change him. Nevertheless he did give the overture to *Struensée* and it would have been no great effort to give the rest. As to *Prométhée*, even if the last part is not in harmony with the rest of it, the work was well worthy the honor of a performance, which the proud society in the Rue Bergère had accorded it. By these refusals Seghers was deprived of the support of two powerful protectors.

Pasdeloup craftily took advantage of the situation. He had plenty of money and, as he knew what the financial situation was, he went to the rehearsals and corrupted the artists. For the most part they were young people in needy circumstances and could not refuse his attractive propositions. He killed Seghers's society and built on its ruins the Société des Jeunes Artistes, which later became the Concerts Populaires.

Pasdeloup was sincerely fond of music but he was a very ordinary musician. He had little of Seghers's feeling and profound comprehension of the art. In Seghers's hands the popular concerts would have become an admirable undertaking, but Pasdeloup, in spite of his zeal and skill, was able to give them only a superficial and deceptive brilliancy. Besides, Seghers would have worked for the development of the French school whom Pasdeloup, with but few exceptions, kept under a bushel until 1870. Among these exceptions were a symphony by Gounod, one by Gouvy and the overture to Berlioz's *Frances-Juges*. Until the misfortunes and calamities of that terrible year the French symphonic school had been repressed and stifled between the Société des Concerts and the Concerts Populaires. Perhaps they were necessary so that this school might be freed and give flight to its fancies.

Chapter XVIII

Rossini

Nowadays it is difficult to form any idea of Rossini's position in our beautiful city of Paris half a century ago. He had retired from active life a long time before, but he had a greater reputation in his idleness than many others in their activity. All Paris sought the honor of being admitted to his magnificent, high-windowed apartment. As the demigod never went out in the evening, his friends were always sure of finding him at home. At one time or another all sorts of social sets rubbed elbows at his great soirees. The most brilliant singers and the most famous virtuosi appeared at these "evenings." The master was surrounded by sycophants, but they did not influence him, for he knew their true worth. He ruled his regular following with the hauteur of a superior being who does not deign to reveal himself to the first comer. It is a question how he came to be held in such honor.

His works, outside of the *Barbier* and *Guillaume Tell*, and some performances of *Moïse*, belonged to the past. They still went to see *Otello* at the Théâtre-Italien, but that was to hear Tamberlick's C diesis. Rossini was under so little illusion that he tried to oppose the effort to have *Semiramide* put into the repertoire at the Opéra. And, nevertheless, the Parisian public actually worshipped him.

This public—I am speaking now of the musical public or what is called that—was divided into two hostile camps. There were the lovers of melody who were in the large majority and included the musical critics; and, on the other side, the subscribers to the Conservatoire and the Maurin, Alard and Amingaud quartets. They were devotees of learned music; "poseurs," others said, who pretended to admire works they did not understand at all.

There was no melody in Beethoven; some even denied that there was any in Mozart. Melody was found, we were told, only in the works of the Italian school, of which Rossini was the leader, and in the school of Herold and Auber, which was descended from the Italian.

The Melodists considered Rossini their standard bearer, a symbol to rally around, even though they had just obtained good prices for his works at the second-hand shops and now permitted them to fall into oblivion.

From some words he let fall during our intimacy I can state that this neglect was painful to him. But it was a just—perhaps too just—retribution for the fatality with which Rossini, doubtless in spite of himself, served as a weapon against Beethoven. The first encounter was at Vienna where the success of *Tancred* crushed forever the dramatic ambitions of the author of *Fidelio*; later, at Paris, they used *Guillaume Tell* in combating the increasing invasion of the symphony and chamber music.

I was twenty when M. and Mme. Viardot introduced me to Rossini. He invited me to his small evening receptions and received me with his usual rather meaningless cordiality. At the end of a month, when he found that I asked to be heard neither as a pianist nor as a composer, he changed his attitude. "Come and see me tomorrow morning," he said. "We can talk then."

I was quick to respond to this flattering invitation and I found a very different Rossini from the one of the evening. He was intensely interested in and open-minded to ideas, which, if they were not advanced, were at least broad and noble. He gave proof of this when Liszt's famous *Messe* was performed for the first time at St. Eustache. He went to its defense in the face of an almost unanimous opposition.

He said to me one day,

"You have written a duet for a flute and clarinet for Dorus and Leroy. Won't you ask them to play it at one of my evenings?"

The two great artists did not have to be urged. Then an unheard of thing happened. As he never had a written programme on such occasions, Rossini managed so that they believed that the duet was his own. It is easy to imagine the success of the piece under these conditions. When the encore was over, Rossini took me to the dining-room and made me sit near him, holding me by the hand so that I could not get away. A procession of fawning admirers passed in front of him. Ah! Master! What a masterpiece! Marvellous!

And when the victim had exhausted the resources of the language in praise, Rossini replied, quietly:

"I agree with you. But the duet wasn't mine; it was written by this gentleman."

Such kindness combined with such ingenuity tells more about the great man than many volumes of commentaries. For Rossini was a great man. The young people of to-day are in no position to judge his works, which were written, as he said himself, for singers and a public who no longer exist.

"I am criticised," he said one day, "for the great *crescendo* in my works. But if I hadn't put the *crescendo* into my works, they would never have been played at the Opéra."

In our day the public are slaves. I have read in the programme of one house, "All marks of approbation will be severely repressed." Formerly, especially in Italy, the public was master and its taste law. As it came before the lights were up, a great overture with a *crescendo* was as necessary as cavatinas, duets and ensembles: they came to hear the singers and not to be present at an opera. In many of his works, especially in *Otello*, Rossini made a great step forward towards realism in opera. In *Moïse* and *Le Siège de Corinthe* (not to mention *Guillaume Tell*) he rose to heights which have not been surpassed in spite of the poverty of the means at his disposal. As Victor Hugo has victoriously demonstrated, such poverty is no obstacle to genius and wealth in them is only an advantage to mediocrity.

I was one of the regular pianists at Rossini's. The others were Stanzieri, a charming young man of whom Rossini was very fond and who lived but a short time, and Diemer, who was also young but already a great artist. One or the other of us would often play at the evening entertainments the slight pieces for the piano which the Master used to write to take up his time. I was only too willing to accompany the singers, when Rossini did not do so himself. He accompanied them admirably for he played the piano to perfection.

Mme. Patti

Unfortunately I was not there the evening that Patti sang for Rossini the first time. We know that after she had sung the aria from *Le Barbier*, he said to her, after the usual compliments,

"Who wrote that aria you just sang?"

I saw him three days afterwards and he hadn't cooled off even then.

"I am fully aware," he said, "that arias should be embellished. That's what they are for. But not to leave a note of them even in the recitatives! That is too much!"

In his irritation he complained that the sopranos persisted in singing this aria which was written for a contralto and did not sing what had been written for the sopranos at all.

On the other hand the diva was irritated as well. She thought the matter over and realized that it would be serious to have Rossini for an enemy. So some days later she went to ask his advice. It was well for her that she took it, for her talent, though brilliant and fascinating, was not as yet fully formed. Two months after this incident, Patti sang the arias from *La Gaza Ladra* and *Semiramide*, with the master as her accompanist. And she combined with her brilliancy the absolute correctness which she always showed afterwards.

Much has been written about the premature interruption of Rossini's career after the appearance of *Guillaume Tell*. It has been compared with Racine's life after *Phèdre*. The failure of *Phèdre* was brutal and cruel, which was added to by the scandalous success of the *Phèdre* of an unworthy rival. Racine's friends, the Port Royalists, did not hesitate to make the most of the opportunity. "You've lost your soul," they told him. "And now you haven't even success." But later, when he took up his pen again, he gave us two masterpieces in *Esther* and *Athalie*.

Rossini was accustomed to success and it was hard for him to run into a half-hearted success when he knew he had surpassed himself. This was doubtless due to the extravagant phraseology of Hippolyte Bis, one of the librettists. But *Guillaume Tell* had its admirers from the start. I heard it spoken of constantly in my childhood. If the work did not appear on the bills of the Opéra, it furnished the amateurs with choice bits.

In my opinion, if Rossini committed suicide as far as his art was concerned, he did so because he had nothing more to say. Rossini was a spoiled child of success and he could not live without it. Such unexpected hostility put an end to a stream which had flowed so abundantly for so long.

The success of his *Soirées Musicales* and his *Stabat* encouraged him. But he wrote nothing more except those slight compositions for the piano and for singing which may be compared to the last vibrations of a sound, as it dies away.

Later—much later—came *La Messe* to which undue importance has been attributed. "*Le Passus,*" one critic wrote, "is the cry of a stricken spirit." La Messe is written with elegance by an assured and expert hand, but that is all. There are no traces of the pen which wrote the second act of *Guillaume Tell*.

Apropos of this second act, it is not, perhaps, generally known that the author had no idea of ending it with a prayer. Insurrections are not usually begun with so serious a song. But at the rehearsals the effect of the unison, *Si parmi nous il est des Traîtres*, was so great that they did not dare to go on beyond it. So they suppressed the real ending, which is now the brilliant entrancing end of the overture. This finale is extant in the library at the Opéra. It would be an interesting experiment to restore it and give this beautiful act its natural conclusion.

Chapter XIX

Jules Massenet

Massenet has been praised indiscriminately—sometimes for his numerous and brilliant powers and sometimes for merits he did not have at all.

I have waited to speak of him until the time when the Académie was ready to replace him,—that is to say, put some one in his place, for great artists are never replaced. Others succeed them with their own individual and different powers, but they do not take their places nevertheless. Malibran has never been replaced, nor Madame Viardot, Madame Carvalho, Talma and Rachel. No one can ever replace Patti, Bartet or Sarah Bernhardt. They could not replace Ingres, Delacroix, Berlioz, or Gounod, and they can never replace Massenet.

It is a question whether he has been accorded his real place. Perhaps his pupils have estimated him at his true worth, but they were grateful for his excellent teaching, and may be rightly suspected of partiality. Others have spoken slightingly of his works and they have applied to him by transposing the words of the celebrated dictum: *Saltavit et placuit.* He sang and wept, so they sought to deprecate him as if there were something reprehensible in an artist's pleasing the public. This notion might seem to have some basis in view of the taste that is affected to-day—a predilection for all that is shocking and displeasing in all the arts, including poetry. Sorcières's epigram—the ugly is beautiful and the beautiful ugly—has become a programme. People are no longer content with merely admiring atrocities, they even speak with contempt of beauties hallowed by time and the admiration of centuries.

The fact remains that Massenet is one of the most brilliant diamonds in our musical crown. No musician has enjoyed so much favor with the public save Auber, whom Massenet did not care for any more than he did for his school, but whom he resembled closely. They were alike in their facility, their amazing fertility, genius, gracefulness, and success. Both composed music which was agreeable to their contemporaries. Both were accused of pandering to their audiences. The answer to this is that both their audiences and the artists had the same tastes and so were in perfect accord.

To-day the revolutionists are the only ones held in esteem by the critics. Well, it may be a fine thing to despise the mob, to struggle against the current, and to compel the mob by force of genius and energy to follow one despite their resistance. Yet one may be a great artist without doing that.

There was nothing revolutionary about Sebastian Bach with his two hundred and fifty cantatas, which were performed as fast as they were written and which were constantly in demand for important occasions. Handel managed the theater where his operas were produced and his oratorios were sung, and they would have indubitably failed, if he had gone against the accustomed taste of his audiences. Haydn wrote to supply the music for Prince Esterhazy's chapel; Mozart was forced to write constantly, and Rossini worked for an intolerant public which would not have allowed one of his operas to be played, if the overture did not contain the great *crescendo* for which he has been so reproached. These were none of them revolutionists, yet they were great musicians.

Another criticism is made against Massenet. He was superficial, they say, and lacked depth. Depth, as we know, is very much the fashion.

It is true that Massenet was not profound, but that is of little consequence. Just as there are many mansions in our Father's house, so there are many in Apollo's. Art is vast. The artist has a perfect right to descend to the nethermost depths and to enter into the inner secrets of the soul, but this right is not a duty.

The artists of Ancient Greece, with all their marvellous works, were not profound. Their marble goddesses were beautiful, and beauty was sufficient.

Our old-time sculptors—Clodion and Coysevox—were not profound; nor were Fragonard, La Tour, nor Marivaux, yet they brought honor to the French school.

All have their value and all are necessary. The rose with its fresh color and its perfume, is, in its way, as precious as the sturdy oak. Art has a place for artists of all kinds, and no one should flatter himself that he is the only one who is capable of covering the entire field of art.

Some, even in treating a familiar subject, have as much dignity as a Roman emperor on his golden throne, but Massenet did not belong to this type. He had charm, attraction and a passionateness that was feverish rather than deep. His melody was wavering and uncertain, oftentimes more a recitative than melody properly so called, and it was entirely his own. It lacks structure and style. Yet how can one resist when he hears Manon at the feet of Des Grieux in the sacristy of Saint-Sulpice, or help being stirred to the depths by such outpourings of love? One cannot reflect or analyze when moved in this way.

After emotional art comes decadent art. But that is of little consequence. Decadence in art is often far from being artistic deterioration.

Massenet's music has one great attraction for me and one that is rare in these days—it is gay. And gaiety is frowned upon in modern music. They criticise Haydn and Mozart for their gaiety, and turn away their faces in shame before the exuberant joyousness with which the *Ninth Symphony* comes to its triumphal close. Long live gloom. Hurrah for boredom! So say our young people. They may live to regret, too late, the lost hours which they might have spent in gaiety.

Massenet's facility was something prodigious. I have seen him sick in bed, in a most uncomfortable position, and still turning off pages of orchestration, which followed one another with disconcerting speed. Too often such facility engenders laziness, but in his case we know what an enormous amount of work he accomplished. He has been criticised as being too prolific. However, that is a quality which belongs only to a master. The artist who produces little may, if he has ability, be an interesting artist, but he will never be a great one.

M. Jules Massenet

In this time of anarchy in art, when all he had to do to conciliate the hostile critics was to array himself with the *fauves*, Massenet set an example of impeccable writing. He knew how to combine modernism with respect for tradition, and he did this at a time when all he had to do was to trample tradition under foot and be proclaimed a genius. Master of his trade as few have ever been, alive to all its difficulties, possessing the most subtle secrets of its technique, he despised the contortions and exaggerations which simple minds confound with the science of music. He followed out the course he had set for himself without any concern for what they might say about him. He was able to adopt within reason the novelties from abroad and he was clever in assimilating them perfectly, yet he presented the spectacle of a thoroughly French artist whom neither the Lorelei of the Rhine nor the sirens of the Mediterranean could lead astray. He was a *virtuoso* of the orchestra, yet he never sacrificed the voices for the instruments, nor did he sacrifice orchestral color for the voices. Finally, he had the greatest gift of all, that of life, a gift which cannot be defined, but which the public always recognizes and which assures the success of works far inferior to his.

Much has been said about the friendship between us—a notion based solely on the demonstrations he showered on me in public—and in public alone. He might have had my friendship, if he had wanted it, and it would have been a devoted friendship, but he did not want it. He told—what I never told—how I got one of his works presented at Weimar, where *Samson* had just been given. What he did not tell was the icy reception he gave me when I brought the news and when I expected an entirely different sort of a reception. From that day on I never intervened again, and I was content to rejoice in his success without expecting any reciprocity on his part, which I knew to be impossible after a confession he made to me one day. My friends and companions in arms were Bizet, Guiraud and Delibes; Massenet was a rival. His high opinion of me, therefore, was the more valuable when he did me the honor of recommending his pupils to study my works. I have brought up this question only to make clear that when I proclaim his great musical importance, I am guided solely by my artistic conscience and that my sincerity cannot be suspected. One word more. Massenet had many imitators; he never imitated anyone.

Chapter XX

Meyerbeer

I

Who would have predicted that the day would come when it would be necessary to come to the defense of the author of *Les Huguenots* and *Le Prophète*, of the man who at one time dominated every stage in Europe by a leadership which was so extraordinary that it looked as though it would never end? I could cite many works in which all the composers of the past are praised without qualification, and Meyerbeer, alone, is accused of numerous faults. However, others have faults, too, and, as I have said elsewhere, but it will stand repeating, it is not the absence of defects but the presence of merits which makes works and men great. It is not always well to be without blemish. A too regular face or too pure a voice lacks expression. If there is no such thing as perfection in this world, it is doubtless because it is not needed.

As I do not belong to that biased school which pretends to see Peter entirely white and Paul utterly black, I do not try to make myself think that the author of *Les Huguenots* had no faults.

The most serious, but the most excusable, is his contempt for prosody and his indifference to the verse entrusted to him. This fault is excusable for the French school of the time, heedless of tradition, set him a bad example. Rossini was, like Meyerbeer, a foreigner, but he was not affected in the same way. He even got fine effects through the combination of musical and textual rhythm. An instance of this is seen in the famous phrase in *Guillaume Tell*:

> Ces jours qu'ils ont osé proscrire,
>
> Je ne les ai pas défendus.
>
> Mon père, tu m'as dû maudire!

If Rossini had not retired at an age when others are just beginning their careers and had given us two or three more works, his illustrious example would have restored the old principles on which French opera had been constructed from the time of Lulli. On the contrary, Auber carried with him an entire generation captivated by Italian music. He even went so far as to put French words into Italian rhythm. The famous duet *Amour sacré de la Patrie* is versified as if the text were *Amore sacro della patria*. This is seen only in reading it, for it is never sung as it is written.

Meyerbeer was, then, excusable to a certain extent, but he abused all indulgence in such matters. In order to preserve intact his musical forms—even in recitatives, which are, as a matter of fact, only declamation set to music—he accented the weak syllables and vice versa; he added words and made unnecessarily false verse, and transformed bad verse into worse prose. He might have avoided all these literary abominations without any harm to the effect by a slight modification of the music. The verses given to musicians were often very bad, for that was the fashion. The versifier thought he had done his duty by his collaborator by giving him verses like this:

> Triomphe que j'aime!
>
> Ta frayeur extrême
>
> Va malgré toi-même
>
> Te livrer à moi!

But when Scribe abandoned his reed-pipes and essayed the lyre, he gave Meyerbeer this,

> J'ai voulu les punir ...Tu les as surpassés!

And Meyerbeer made it,

> J'ai voulu les punir ... Et tu les as surpassés!

which was hardly encouraging.

Meyerbeer had other manias as well. Perhaps the most notable was to give to the voice musical schemes which belong by rights to the instruments. So in the first act of *Le Prophète*, after the chorus sings, *Veille sur nous*, instead of stopping to breathe and prepare for the following phrase, he makes it repeat abruptly, *Sur nous! Sur nous!* in unison with the orchestral notes which are, to say the least, *a ritornello.*

Again, in the great cathedral scene, instead of letting the orchestra bring out through the voices the musical expression of Fidès sobs: *Et toi, tu ne me connais pas*, he puts both the instruments and the voices in the same time and on words which do not harmonize with the music at all.

I need not speak of his immoderate love for the bassoon, an admirable instrument, but one which it is hardly prudent to abuse.

But so far we have spoken only of trifles. Meyerbeer's music, as a witty woman once remarked to me, is like stage scenery — it should not be scrutinized too closely. It would be hard to find a better characterization. Meyerbeer belonged to the theater and sought above everything else theatrical effects. But that does not mean that he was indifferent to details. He was a wealthy man and he used to indemnify the theaters for the extra expense he occasioned them. He multiplied rehearsals by trying different versions with the orchestra so as to choose between them. He did not cast his work in bronze, as so many do, and present it to the public *ne varietur*. He was continually feeling his way, recasting, and seeking the better which very often was the enemy of good. As the result of his continual researches he too frequently turned good ideas into inferior ones. Note for example, in *L'Etoile du Nord*, the passage, *Enfants de l'Ukraine fils du désert.* The opening passage is lofty, determined and picturesque, but it ends most disagreeably.

He always lived alone with no fixed place of abode. He was at Spa in the summer and on the Mediterranean in the winter; in large cities only as business drew him. He had no financial worries and he lived only to continue his Penelope-like work, which showed a great love of perfection, although he did not find the best way of attaining it. They have tried to place this conscientious artist in the list of seekers of success, but such men are not ordinarily accustomed to work like this.

Since I have used the word artist, it is proper to stop for a moment. Unlike Gluck and Berlioz, who were greater artists than musicians, Meyerbeer was more a musician than an artist. As a result, he often used the most refined and learned means to achieve a very ordinary artistic result. But there is no reason why he should be brought to task for results which they do not even remark in the works of so many others.

Meyerbeer was the undisputed leader in the operatic world when Robert Schumann struck the first blow at his supremacy. Schumann was ignorant of the stage, although he had made one unfortunate venture there. He did not appreciate that there is more than one way to practise the art of music. But he attacked Meyerbeer, violently, for his bad taste and Italian tendencies, entirely forgetting that when Mozart, Beethoven, and Weber did work for the stage they were strongly drawn towards Italian art. Later, the Wagnerians wanted to oust Meyerbeer from the stage and make a place for themselves, and they got credit for some of Schumann's harsh criticisms,—this, too, despite the fact that at the beginning of the skirmish Schumann and the Wagnerians got along about as well as Ingres and Delacroix and their schools. But they united against the common enemy and the French critics followed. The critics entirely neglected Berlioz's opinion, for, after opposing Meyerbeer for a long time, he admitted him among the gods and in his *Traité d'Instrumentation* awarded him the crown of immortality.

Parenthetically, if there is a surprising page in the history of music it is the persistent affectation of classing Berlioz and Wagner together. They had nothing in common save their great love of art and their distrust of established forms. Berlioz abhorred enharmonic modulations, dissonances resolved indefinitely one after another, continuous melody and all current practices of futuristic music. He carried this so far that he claimed that he understood nothing in the prelude to *Tristan*, which was certainly a sincere claim since, almost simultaneously, he hailed the overture of *Lohengrin*, which is conceived in an entirely different manner, as a masterpiece. He did not admit that the voice should be sacrificed and relegated to the rank of a simple unit of the orchestra. Wagner, for his part, showed at his best an elegance and artistry of pen which may be searched for in vain in Berlioz's work. Berlioz opened to the orchestra the doors of a new world. Wagner hurled himself into this unknown country and found numerous lands to till there. But what dissimilarities there are in the styles of the two men! In their methods of treating the orchestra and the voices, in their musical architectonics, and in their conception of opera!

In spite of the great worth of *Les Troyens* and *Benvenuto Cellini*, Berlioz shone brightest in the concert hall; Wagner is primarily a man of the theater. Berlioz showed clearly in *Les Troyens* his intention of approaching Gluck, while Wagner freely avowed his indebtedness to Weber, and particularly to the score of *Euryanthe*. He might have added that he owed something to Marschner, but he never spoke of that.

The more we study the works of these two men of genius, the more we are impressed by the tremendous difference between them. Their resemblance is simply one of those imaginary things which the critics too often mistake for a reality. The critics once found local color in Rossini's *Semiramide*!

Hans de Bülow once said to me in the course of a conversation,

"After all Meyerbeer was a man of genius."

If we fail to recognize Meyerbeer's genius, we are not only unjust but also ungrateful. In every sense, in his conception of opera, in his treatment of orchestration, in his handling of choruses, even in stage setting, he gave us new principles by which our modern works have profited to a large extent.

Théophile Gautier was no musician, but he had a fine taste in music and he judged Meyerbeer as follows:

"In addition to eminent musical talents, Meyerbeer had a highly developed instinct for the stage. He goes to the heart of a situation, follows closely the meanings of the words, and observes both the historical and local color of his subject.... Few composers have understood opera so well."

The success of the Italian school appeared to have utterly ruined this understanding and care for local and historical color. Rossini in the last act of *Otello* and in *Guillaume Tell* began its renaissance with a boldness for which he deserves credit, but it was left to Meyerbeer to restore it to its former glory.

It is impossible to deny his individuality. The amalgamation of his Germanic tendencies with his Italian education and his French preferences formed an ore of new brilliancy and new depth of tone. His style resembled none other. Fétis, his great admirer and friend and the famous director of the Conservatoire at Brussels, insisted, and with reason, on this distinction. His style was characterized by the importance of the rhythmic element. His ballet music owes much of its excellence to the picturesque variety of the rhythms.

Instead of the long involved overture he gave us the short distinctive prelude which has been so successful. The preludes of *Robert* and *Les Huguenots* were followed by the preludes of *Lohengrin, Faust, Tristan, Romeo, La Traviata, Aïda*, and many others which are less famous. Verdi in his last two works and Richard Strauss in *Salome* went even farther and suppressed the prelude—a none too agreeable surprise. It is like a dinner without soup.

Meyerbeer gave us a foretaste of the famous *leit-motif*. We find it in *Robert* in the theme of the ballad, which the orchestra plays again while Bertram goes towards the back of the stage. This should indicate to the listener his satanic character. We find it in the Luther chant in *Les Huguenots* and also in the dream of *Le Prophète* during Jean's recitative. Here the orchestra with its modulated tone predicts the future splendor of the cathedral scene, while a lute plays low notes, embellished by a delicate weaving in of the violins, and produces a remarkable and unprecedented effect. He introduced on the stage the ensembles of wind instruments (I do not mean the brass) which are so frequent in Mozart's great concertos. An illustration of this is the entrance of Alice in the second act of *Robert*. An echo of this is found in Elsa's entrance in the second act of *Lohengrin*. Another illustration is the entrance of Berthe and Fidès in the beginning of the *Le Prophète*. In this case the author indicated a pantomime. This is never played and so this pretty bit loses all its significance.

Meyerbeer ventured to use combinations in harmony which were considered rash at that time. They pretend that the sensitiveness of the ear has been developed since then, but in reality it has been dulled by having to undergo the most violent discords.

The beautiful "progression" of the exorcism in the fourth act of *Le Prophète* was not accepted without some difficulty. I can still see Gounod seated at a piano singing the debated passage and trying to convince a group of recalcitrant listeners of its beauty.

Meyerbeer developed the rôle of the English horn, which up to that time had been used only rarely and timidly, and he also introduced the bass clarinet into the orchestra. But the two instruments, as he used them, still appeared somewhat unusual. They were objects of luxury, strangers of distinction which one saluted respectfully and which played no great part. Under Wagner's management they became a definite part of the household and, as we know, brought in a wealth of coloring.

It is an open question whether it was Meyerbeer or Scribe who planned the amazing stage setting in the cathedral scene in *Le Prophète*. It must have been Meyerbeer, for Scribe was not temperamentally a revolutionist, and this scene was really revolutionary. The brilliant procession with its crowd of performers which goes across the stage through the nave into the choir, constantly keeping its distance from the audience, is an impressive, realistic and beautiful scene. But directors who go to great expense for the costumes cannot understand why the procession should file anywhere except before the footlights as near the audience as possible, and it is extremely difficult to get any other method of procedure.

Furthermore, the amusing idea of the skating ballet was due to Meyerbeer. At the time there was an amusing fellow in Paris who had invented roller skates and who used to practise his favorite sport on fine evenings on the large concrete surfaces of the Place de la Concorde. Meyerbeer saw him and got the idea of the famous ballet. In the early days of the opera it certainly was charming to see the skaters come on accompanied by a pretty chorus and a rhythm from the violins regulated by that of the dancers. But the performance began at seven and ended at midnight. Now they begin at eight and to gain the hour they had to accelerate the pace. So the chorus in question was sacrificed. That was bad for *Les Huguenots*. The author tried to make a good deal out of the last act with its beautiful choruses in the church—a development of the Luther chant—and the terror of the approaching massacre. But this act has been cut, mutilated and made generally unrecognizable. They even go so far in some of the foreign houses as to suppress it entirely.

I once saw the last act in all its integrity and with six harps accompanying the famous trio. We shall never see the six harps again, for Garnier, instead of reproducing exactly the placing of the orchestra in the old Opéra, managed so well in the new one that they are unable to put in the six harps of old or the four drums with which Meyerbeer got such surprising effects in *Robert* and *Le Prophète*. I believe, however, that recent improvements have averted this disaster in a certain measure, and that there is now a place for the drums. But we shall never hear the six harps again.

We must say something of the genesis of Meyerbeer's works, for in many instances this was curious and few people know about it.

II

We might like to see works spring from the author's brain as complete as Minerva was when she sprang from Jove's, but that is infrequently the case. When we study the long series of operas which Gluck wrote, we are surprised to meet some things which we recognize as having seen before in the masterpieces which immortalize his name. And often the music is adapted to entirely different situations in the changed form. The words of a follower become the awesome prophecy of a high priest. The trio in *Orphée* with its tender love and expressions of perfect happiness fairly trembles with accents of sorrow. The music had been written for an entirely different situation which justified them. Massenet has told us that he borrowed right and left from his unpublished score, *La Coupe du Roi de Thulé*. That is what Gluck did with his *Elena e Paride* which had little success. I may as well confess that one of the ballets in *Henry VIII* came from the finale of an opéra-comique in one act. This work was finished and ready to go to rehearsal when the whole thing was stopped because I had the audacity to assert to Nestor Roqueplan, the director of Favart Hall, that Mozart's *Le Nozze di Figaro* was a masterpiece.

Meyerbeer, even more than anyone, tried not to lose his ideas and the study of their transformation is extremely interesting. One day Nuitter, the archivist at the Opéra, learned of an important sale of manuscripts in Berlin. He attended the sale and brought back a lot of Meyerbeer's rough drafts which included studies for a *Faust* that the author never finished. These fragments give no idea what the piece would have been. We see Faust and Mephistopheles walking in Hell. They come to the Tree of Human Knowledge on the banks of the Styx and Faust picks the fruit. From this detail it is easy to imagine that the libretto is bizarre. The authorship of this amazing libretto is unknown, but it is not strange that Meyerbeer soon abandoned it. From this still-born *Faust*, Scribe, at the request of the author, constructed *Robert le Diable*. An aria sung by Faust on the banks of the Styx becomes the *Valse Infernale*.

The necessity of utilizing pre-existing fragments explains some of the incoherence of this incomprehensible piece. It also explains the creation of Bertram, half man, half devil, who was invented as a substitute for Mephistopheles. The fruit of the Tree of Human Knowledge became the *Rameau Vénérée* in the third act, and the beautiful religious scene in the fifth act, which has no relation to the action, is a transposition of the Easter scene.

So Scribe should not be blamed for making a poor piece when he had so many difficulties to contend with. He must have lost his head a little for Robert's mother was called Berthe in the first act and Rosalie in the third. However, the answer might be that she changed her name when she became religious.

Later, Scribe was put to another no less difficult test with *L'Etoile du Nord*. When Meyerbeer was the conductor at the Berlin Opéra, he wrote on command *Le Camp de Silésie* with Frederick the Great as the hero and Jenny Lind as the musical star. As we know, Frederick was a musician, for he both composed music and played the flute, while Jenny Lind, the Swedish nightingale, was a great singer. A contest between the nightingale and the flute was sure to follow or theatrical instinct is a vain phrase. But in the piece Scribe created, Peter the Great took Frederick the Great's place and to give a motive for the grace notes in the last act it was necessary for the terrible Tsar, a half savage barbarian, to learn to play the flute.

It is not worth while telling how the Tsar took lessons on the flute from a young pastry cook who came on the stage with a basket of cakes on his head; how the cook later became a lord, and many other details of this absurd play. It is permitted to be absurd on the stage, if it is done so that the absurdity is forgotten. But in this instance it was impossible to forget the absurdities. The extravagance of the libretto led the musician into many unfortunate things. This extremely interesting score is very uneven, but there are a thousand details worth the attention of the professional musician. Beauty even appears in the score at moments, and there are charming and picturesque bits, as well as puerilities and shocking vulgarities.

Public curiosity was aroused for a long time by clever advance notices and had reached a high pitch when *L'Etoile du Nord* appeared. The work was carried by the exceptional talents of Bataille and Caroline Duprez and was enormously successful at the start, but this success has grown steadily less. Faure and Madame Patti gave some fine performances in London. We shall probably never see their equal again, and it is not desirable that we should either from the standpoint of art or of the author.

Les Huguenots was not an opera pieced together out of others, but it did not reach the public as the author wrote it. At the beginning of the first act there was a game of cup and ball on which the author had set his heart. But the balls had to strike at the exact moment indicated in the score and the players never succeeded in accomplishing that. The passage had to be suppressed but it is preserved in the library at the Opéra. They also had to suppress the part of Catherine de Medici who should preside at the conference where the massacre of St. Bartholomew was planned. Her part was merged with that of St. Pris. They also suppressed the first scene in the last act, where Raoul, disheveled and covered with blood, interrupted the ball and upset the merriment by announcing the massacre to the astonished dancers.

But it is a question whether we should believe the legend that the great duet, the climax of the whole work, was improvised during the rehearsals at the request of Norritt and Madame Falcon. It is hard to believe that. The work, as is well known, was taken from Merimee's *Chronique du règne de Charles IX*. This scene is in the romance and it is almost impossible that Meyerbeer had no idea of putting it into his opera. More probably the people at the theatre wanted the act to end with the blessing of the daggers, and the author with his duet in his portfolio only had to take it out to satisfy his interpreters. A beautiful scene like this with its sweep and pleasing innovation is not written hastily. This duet should be heard when the author's intentions and the nuances which make a part of the idea are respected and not replaced by inventions in bad taste which they dare to call traditions. The real traditions have been lost and this admirable scene has lost its beauty.

The manner in which the duet ends has not been noted sufficiently. Raoul's phrase, *God guard our days. God of our refuge!* remains in suspense and the orchestra brings it to an end, the first example of a practice used frequently in modern works.

We do not know how Meyerbeer got his idea of putting the schismatic John Huss on the stage under the name of John of Leyden. Whether this idea was original with him or was suggested by Scribe, who made a fantastic person out of John, we do not know. We only know that the rôle of the prophet's mother was originally intended for Madame Stoltz, but she had left the Opéra. Meyerbeer heard Madame Pauline Viardot at Vienna and found in her his ideal, so he created the redoubtable rôle of Fidès for her. The part of Jean was given to the tenor Roger, the star of the Opéra-Comique, and he played and sang it well. Levasseur, the Marcel of *Les Huguenots* and the Bertram of *Robert*, played the part of Zacharie.

Le Prophète was enormously successful in spite of the then powerful censer-bearers of the Italian school. We now see its defects rather than its merits. Meyerbeer is criticised for not putting into practice theories he did not know and no account is taken of his fearlessness, which was great for that period. No one else could have drawn the cathedral scene with such breadth of stroke and extraordinary brilliancy. The paraphrase of *Domine salvum fac regem* reveals great ingenuity. His method of treating the organ is wonderful, and his idea of the ritournello *Sur le Jeu de hautbois* is charming. This precedes and introduces the children's chorus, and is constructed on a novel theme which is developed brilliantly by the choruses, the orchestra and the organ combined. The repetition of the *Domine Salvum* at the end of the scene, which bursts forth abruptly in a different key, is full of color and character.

Meyerbeer, Composer of *Les Huguenots*

III

The story of *Le Pardon de Ploërmel* is interesting. It was first called *Dinorah*, a name which Meyerbeer picked up abroad. But Meyerbeer liked to change the titles of his operas several times in the course of the rehearsals in order to keep public curiosity at fever heat. He had the notion of writing an opéra-comique in one act, and he asked his favorite collaborators, Jules Barbier and Michael Carré, for a libretto. They produced *Dinorah* in three scenes and with but three characters. The music was written promptly and was given to Perrin, the famous director, whose unfortunate influence soon made itself felt. A director's first idea at that time was to demand changes in the piece given him. "A single act by you, Master? Is that permissible? What can we put on after that? A new work by Meyerbeer should take up the entire evening." That was the way the insidious director talked, and there was all the more chance of his being listened to as the author was possessed by a mania for retouching and making changes. So Meyerbeer took the score to the Mediterranean where he spent the winter. The next spring he brought back the work developed into three acts with choruses and minor characters. Besides these additions he had written the words which Barbier and Carré should have done.

The rehearsals were tedious. Meyerbeer wanted Faure and Madame Carvalho in the leading rôles but one was at the Opéra-Comique and the other at her own house, the Théâtre-Lyrique. The work went back and forth from the Place Favart to the Place du Châtelet. But the author's hesitancy was at bottom only a pretext. What he wanted was to secure a postponement of Limnander's opera *Les Blancs et les Bleus*. The action of this work and of *Dinorah*, as well, took place in Brittany. In the hope of being Meyerbeer's choice, both theatres turned poor Limnander away. Finally, *Dinorah* fell to the Opéra-Comique. After long hard work, which the author demanded, Madame Cabel and MM. Faure and Sainte-Foix gave a perfect performance.

There was a good deal of criticism of having the hunter, the reaper, and the shepherd sing a prayer together at the beginning of the third act. This was not considered theatrical; to-day that is a virtue.

There was a good deal of talk about *L'Africanne*, which had been looked for for a long time and which seemed to be almost legendary and mysterious; it still is for that matter. The subject of the opera was unknown. All that was known was that the author was trying to find an interpreter and could get none to his liking.

Then Marie Cruvelli, a German singer with an Italian training, appeared. With her beauty and prodigious voice she shone like a meteor in the theatrical firmament. Meyerbeer found his Africanne realized in her and at his request she was engaged at the Opéra. Her engagement was made the occasion for a brilliant revival of *Les Huguenots* and Meyerbeer wrote new ballet music for it. To-day we have no idea of what *Les Huguenots* was then. Then the author went back to his Africanne and went to work again. He used to go to see the brilliant singer about it nearly every day, when she suddenly announced that she was going to leave the stage to become the Comtesse Vigier! Meyerbeer was discouraged and he threw his unfinished manuscript into a drawer where it stayed until Marie Sass had so developed her voice and talent that he made up his mind to entrust the rôle of Sélika to her. He wanted Faure for the rôle of Nelusko and he was already at the Opéra, so he had the management engage Naudin, the Italian tenor, as well.

But Scribe had died during the long period which had elapsed since the marriage of the Comtesse Vigier. Meyerbeer was now left to himself, and too much inclined to revisions of every kind as he was, re-made the piece to his fancy. When it was completed—it didn't resemble anything and the author planned to finish it at the rehearsals.

As we know, Meyerbeer died suddenly. He realized that he was dying and as he knew how necessary his presence was for a performance of *L'Africanne* he forbade its appearance. But his prohibition was only verbal as he could no longer write. The public was impatiently awaiting *L'Africanne*, so they went ahead with it.

When Perrin and his nephew du Locle opened the package of manuscripts Meyerbeer had left, they were stupefied at finding no *L'Africanne*.

"Never mind," said Perrin, "the public wants an *Africanne* and it shall have one."

He summoned Fétis, Meyerbeer's enthusiastic admirer, and the three, Fétis, Perrin and du Locle, managed to evolve the opera we know from the scraps the author had left in disorder. They did not accomplish this, however, without considerable difficulty, without some incoherences, numerous suppressions and even additions. Perrin was the inventor of the wonderful map on which Sélika recognized Madagascar. They took the characters there in order to justify the term Africanne applied to the heroine. They also introduced the Brahmin religion to Madagascar in order to avoid moving the characters to India where the fourth act should take place. The first performance was imminent when they found that the work was too long. So they cut out an original ballet where a savage beat a tom-tom, and they cut and fitted together mercilessly. In the last act Sélika, alone and dying, should see the paradise of the Brahmins appear as in a vision. But Faure wanted to appear again at the finale, so they had to adapt a bit taken from the third act and suppress the vision. This is the reason why Nelusko succumbs so quickly to the deadly perfume of the poisonous flowers, while Sélika resists so long. The riturnello of Sélika's aria, which should be performed with lowered curtain as the queen gazes over the sea and at the departing vessel far away on the horizon, became a vehicle for encores—the last thing that was ever in Meyerbeer's mind. But the worst was the liberty Fétis took in retouching the orchestration. As a compliment to Adolph Sax he substituted a saxaphone for the bass clarinet which the author indicated. This resulted in the suppression of that part of the aria beginning *O Paradis sorti de l'onde* as the saxophone did not produce a good effect. Fétis also allowed Perrin to make over a bass solo into a chorus, the Bishop's Chorus. The great vocal range in this is poorly adapted for a chorus. Some barbarous modulations are certainly apocryphal....

We are unable to imagine what *L'Africanne* would have been if Scribe had lived and the authors had put it into shape. The work we have is illogical and incomplete. The words are simply monstrous and Scribe certainly would not have kept them. This is the case in the passage in the great duet:

O ma Sélika, vous régnez sur mon âme!

—Ah! ne dis pas ces mots brûlante!

Ils m'égarent moi-même....

The music stitched to this impossible piece, however, had its admirers—even fanatical admirers—so great was the prestige of the author's name at the time of its appearance. We must not forget that there are, indeed, some beautiful pages in this chaos. The religious ceremony in the fourth act and the Brahmin recitative accompanied by the *pizzicati* of the bass may be mentioned as an indication of this. The latter passage is not in favor, however; they play it down without conviction and so deprive it of all its strength and majesty.

I said, at the beginning of this study, that we were ungrateful to Meyerbeer, and this ingratitude is double on the part of France, for he loved her. He only had to say the word to have any theatre in Europe opened to him, yet he preferred to them all the Opéra at Paris and even the Opéra-Comique where the choruses and orchestra left much to be desired. When he did work for Paris after he had given *Margherita d'Anjou* and *Le Crociato* in Italy, he was forced to accommodate himself to French taste just as Rossini and Donizetti were. The latter wrote for the Opéra-Comique *La Fille du Régiment*, a military and patriotic work, and its dashing and glorious *Salut à la France* has resounded through the whole world. Foreigners do not take so much pains in our day, and France applauds *Die Meistersinger* which ends with a hymn to German art. Such is progress!

Something must be said of a little known score, *Struensée*, which was written for a drama which was so weak that it prevented the music gaining the success it deserved. The composer showed himself in this more artistic than in anything else he did. It should have been heard at the Odéon with another piece written by Jules Barbier on the same subject. The overture used to appear in the concerts as did the polonnaise, but like the overture to *Guillaume Tell*, they have disappeared. These overtures are not negligible. The overture to *Guillaume Tell* is notable for the unusual invention of the five violoncellos and its storm with its original beginning, to say nothing of its pretty pastoral. The fine depth of tone in the exordium of *Struensée* and the fugue development in the main theme are also not to be despised. But all that, we are told, is lacking in elevation and depth. Possibly; but it is not always necessary to descend to Hell and go up to Heaven. There is certainly more music in these overtures than in Grieg's *Peer Gynt* which has been dinned into our ears so much.

But enough of this. I must stop with the operas, for to consider the rest of his music would necessitate a study of its own and that would take us too far afield. My hope is that these lines may repair an unnecessary injustice and redirect the fastidious who may read them to a great musician whom the general public has never ceased to listen to and applaud.

Chapter XXI

Jacques Offenbach

It is dangerous to prophesy. Not long ago I was speaking of Offenbach, trying to do justice to his marvellous natural gifts and deploring his squandering them. And I was imprudent enough to say that posterity would never know him. Now posterity is proving that I was wrong, for Offenbach is coming back into fashion. Our contemporaneous composers forget that Mozart, Beethoven and Sebastian Bach knew how to laugh at times. They distrust all gaiety and declare it unesthetic. As the good public cannot resign itself to getting along without gaiety, it goes to operetta and turns naturally to Offenbach who created it and furnished an inexhaustible supply. My phrase is not exaggerated, for Offenbach hardly dreamed of creating an art. He was endowed with a genius for the comic and an abundance of melody, but he had no thought of doing anything beyond providing material for the theatre he managed at the time. As a matter of fact he was almost its only author.

He was unable to rid himself of his Germanic influences and so corrupted the taste of an entire generation by his false prosody, which has been incorrectly considered originality. In addition he was lacking in taste. At the time they affected a dreadful mannerism of always stopping on the next to the last note of a passage, whether or not it was associated with a mute syllable. This mannerism had no purpose beyond indicating to the audience the end of a passage and giving the claque the signal to applaud. Offenbach did not belong to that heroic strain to which success is the least of its cares. So he adopted this mannerism, and often his ingeniously turned and charming couplets are ruined by this silly absurdity now gone out of fashion.

Furthermore, he wrote badly, for his early education was neglected. If the *Tales of Hoffman* shows traces of a practised pen, it is because Guiraud finished the score and went out of his way to remedy some of the author's mistakes. Leaving aside the bad prosody and the minor defects in taste, we have left a work which shows a wealth of invention, melody, and sparkling fancy comparable to Grétry's.

Grétry was no more a great musician than Offenbach, for he also wrote badly. The essential difference between the two was the care, not only in his prosody but also in his declamation, which Grétry tried to reproduce musically with all possible exactness. He overshot the mark in this for he did not see that in singing the expression of a note is modified by the harmonic scheme which accompanies it. It must be recognized, in addition, that many times Grétry was carried away by his melodic inventiveness and forgot his own principles so that he relegated his care for declamation to second place.

What hurt Grétry was his unbounded conceit, with which Offenbach, to his credit, was never afflicted. As an indication of this, he dared to write in his advice to young musicians:

"Those who have genius will make opéra-comique like mine; those who have talent will write opera like Gluck's; while those who have neither genius nor talent, will write symphonies like Haydn's."

However, he tried to make an opera like Gluck's and in spite of his great efforts and his interesting inventions, he could not equal the work of his formidable rival.

Although he was not a great musician, Offenbach had a surprising natural instinct and made here and there curious discoveries in harmony. In speaking of these discoveries I must go slightly into the theory of harmony and resign myself to being understood only by those of my readers who are more or less musicians. In a slight work, *Daphnis et Chloé*, Offenbach risked a dominant eleventh without either introduction or conclusion—an extraordinary audacity at the time. A short course in harmony is necessary for the understanding of this. We must start with the fact that, theoretically, all dissonances must be introduced and concluded, which we cannot explain here, but this leading up to and away from have for their purpose softening the harshness of the dissonance which was greatly feared in bygone times. Take if you please, the simple key of C natural. *Do* is the keynote, *sol* is the dominant. Place on this dominant two-thirds—*si-re*—and you have the perfect dominant chord. Add a third *fa* and you have the famous dominant seventh, a dissonance which to-day seems actually agreeable. Not so long ago they thought that they ought to prepare for the dissonance. In the Sixteenth Century it was not regarded as admissible at all, for one hears the two notes *si* and *fa* simultaneously and this seems intolerable to the ear. They used to call it the *Diabolus in musica*.

Palestrina was the first to employ it in an anthem. Opinions differ on this, and certain students of harmony pretend that the chord which Palestrina used only has the appearance of the dominant seventh. I do not concur in this view. But however the case may be, the glory of unchaining the devil in music belongs to Montreverde. That was the beginning of modern music.

Later, a new third was superimposed and they dared the chord *sol-si-re-fa-la*. The inventor is unknown, but Beethoven seems to have been the first to make any considerable use of it. He used the chord in such a way that, in spite of its current use to-day, in his works it appears like something new and strange. This chord imposes its characteristics on the second *motif* of the first part of the *Symphony in C minor*. This is what gives such amazing charm to the long colloquy between the flute, the oboe and the clarinets, which always surprises and arouses the listener, in the *andante* of the same symphony. Fétis in his *Traité d'Harmonie* inveighed against this delightful passage. He admits that people like it, but, according to him, the author had no right to write it and the listener has no right to admire it. Scholars often have strange ideas.

Then Richard Wagner came along and the reign of the ninth dominant took the place of the seventh. That is what gives *Tannhauser*, and *Lohengrin* their exciting character, which is dear to those who demand in music above everything else the pleasure due to shocks to the nervous system. Imitators have fallen foul of this easy procedure, and with a laughable naïveté imagine that in this way they can easily equal Wagner. And they have succeeded in making this valuable chord absolutely banal.

Jacques Offenbach

By adding still another third we have the dominant eleventh. Offenbach used this, but it has played but a small part since then. Beyond that we cannot go, for a third more and we are back to the basic note, two octaves away.

But innovations in harmony are rare in Offenbach's work. What makes him interesting is his fertility in invention of melodies and few have equaled him in this. He improvised constantly and with incredible rapidity. His manuscripts give the impression of having been done with the point of a needle. There is nothing useless anywhere in them. He used abbreviations as much as he could and the simplicity of his harmony helped him here. As a result he was able to produce his light works in an exceedingly short time.

He had the luck to attach Madame Ugalde to his company. Her powers had already begun to decline but she was still brilliant. While she was giving a spectacular revival of *Orphée aux Enfers*, he wrote *Les Bavards* for her. He was inspired by the hope of an unusual interpretation and he so surpassed himself that he produced a small masterpiece. A revival of this work would certainly be successful if that were possible, but the peculiar merits of the creatrix of the rôle would be necessary and I do not see her like anywhere.

It is strange but true that Offenbach lost all his good qualities as soon as he took himself seriously. But he was not the only case of this in the history of music. Cramer and Clementi wrote studies and exercises which are marvels of style, but their sonatas and concertos are tiresome in their mediocrity. Offenbach's works which were given at the Opéra-Comique—*Robinson Crusoé*, *Vert-Vert*, and *Fantasio* are much inferior to *La Chanson de Fortunio*, *La Belle Hélène* and many other justly famous operettas. There have been several unprofitable revivals of *La Belle Hélène*. This is due to the fact that the rôle of Hélène was designed for Mlle. Schneider. She was beautiful and talented and had an admirable mezzo-soprano voice. The slight voice of the ordinary singer of operetta is insufficient for the part. Furthermore, traditions have sprung up. The comic element has been suppressed and the piece has been denatured by this change. In Germany they conceived the idea of playing this farce seriously with an archaic stage setting!

Jacques Offenbach will become a classic. While this may be unexpected, what doesn't happen? Everything is possible—even the impossible.

Chapter XXII

Their Majesties

Queen Victoria did me the honor to receive me twice at Windsor Castle, and Queen Alexandra paid me the same honor at Buckingham Palace in London. The first time I saw Queen Victoria I was presented to her by the Baroness de Caters. She was the daughter of Lablache and had one of the most beautiful voices and the greatest talent that I have ever known. This charming woman had been left a widow and so she became an artist, appearing in concerts and giving singing lessons. At the time of which I speak she was teaching Princess Beatrice, now the mother-in-law of the King of Spain. In all the glory of the freshness of youth, the Princess was endowed with a charming voice which the Baroness guided perfectly. The Princess received Madame de Caters and myself with a gracefulness which was increased by her unusual bashfulness. Her Majesty, in the meantime, was finishing her luncheon. I was somewhat apprehensive through having heard of the coldness which the Queen affected at this sort of audience, so I was more than surprised when she came in with both hands extended to take mine and when she addressed me with real cordiality. She was very fond of Baroness de Caters and that was the secret of the reception which put me at my ease at once.

Her Majesty wanted to hear me play the organ (there is an excellent one in the chapel at Windsor), and then the piano. Finally, I had the honor of accompanying the Princess as she sang the aria from *Etienne Marcel*. Her Royal Highness sang with great clearness and distinctness, but it was the first time she had sung before her august mother and she was frightened almost to death. The Queen was so delighted that some days later, without my being told of it, she summoned to Windsor, Madame Gye, wife of the manager of Covent Garden,—the famous singer Albani—to ask to have *Etienne Marcel* staged at her own theatre. The Queen's wish was not granted.

I returned to Windsor seventeen years later, in company with Johann Wolf, who was for many years Queen Victoria's chosen violinist. We dined at the palace, and, if we did not enjoy the distinction of sitting at the royal table, we were nevertheless in good company with the young princesses, daughters of the Duke of Connaught. We were lodged at a hotel for the honor of sleeping at the Castle was reserved for very important personages—an honor which need not be envied, for the sleeping apartments are really servants' rooms. But etiquette decrees it.

Dinner was over, and princes in full uniform and princesses in elaborate evening dress stood about, waiting for her Majesty's appearance. I was heartbroken when I saw her enter, for she was almost carried by her Indian servant and obviously could not walk alone. But once seated at a small table, she was just as she had been before, with her wonderful charm, her simple manner and her musical voice. Only her white hair bore witness to the years that had passed. She asked me about *Henri VIII*, which was being given for the second time at Covent Garden, and I explained to her that in my desire to give the piece the local color of its times I had been ferreting about in the royal library at Buckingham Palace, to which my friend, the librarian, had given me access. And I also told how I had found in a great collection of manuscripts of the Sixteenth Century an exquisitely fine theme arranged for the harpsichord, which served as the framework for the opera—I used it later for the march I wrote for the coronation of King Edward. The Queen was much interested in music in general and she appeared to be especially pleased in this discussion. His Highness the Duke of Connaught wrote me that she had spoken of it several times.

The musical library at Buckingham Palace is most remarkable and it is a pity that access to it is not easier. Among other things, there are the manuscripts of Handel's oratorios, written for the most part with disconcerting rapidity. His *Messiah* was composed in fifteen days! The rudimentary instrumentation of the time made such speed possible, yet who is there to-day who could write all those fugue choruses with such speed? The fugue manner, which seems laborious to us, was current at the time and they were practised in it. The library also contains works of Handel's contemporaries, which are executed with the same mastery. We cannot say whether they were written with the same rapidity as Handel's, but it is easy to see that there was a general ability to do so, just as now it is a matter of common attainment to produce complicated orchestral effects, the possibility of which the old masters had no conception. What made Handel superior to his rivals was the romantic and picturesque side of his works; probably also, his prodigious and unvarying fertility.

The last word has been said about Queen Victoria, yet the peculiar charm which radiated from her personality cannot be too highly praised. She seemed the personification of England. When she passed on, it seemed as though a great void were left. All King Edward's splendid qualities were necessary to take her place, combined with the effect of the world's surprise at discovering a great king where they had expected to see only a brilliant prince who had been a constant lover of pomp and pleasure.

I was later admitted to Buckingham Palace to play with Josef Hollman, the violinist, before Queen Alexandra. We both were eager for this opportunity which we were told was impossible. The Queen was very busy, and, in addition, she was in mourning for the successive deaths of her father and mother, the King and Queen of Denmark. Suddenly, however, we learned that she would receive us. She was pale and appeared to be feeble, but she received us with the utmost cordiality. She spoke to me about her mother, whom I had seen at Copenhagen with her sisters the Empress Dowager of Russia, and the Princess of Hanover whom politics deprived of a crown which was hers by right. I have a very pleasant recollection of this visit. I do not know how it happened but I remained speechless at this lead from the Queen. She brought the subject up a second time and my timidity still prevented my responding. I ought to have had many things to say to one so obviously eager to listen. This Queen of Denmark, with her eighty years, was the most delightful old lady imaginable. Erect, slight, alert of mind and unfaltering of speech, she reminded me vividly of my maternal great-aunt, that extraordinary woman, who gave me my first notions of things and directed my hand on the keys so well.

A singer whom I had never seen or heard of, but of whom I had heard poor reports, had written Queen Louise that I wanted to accompany her to court. The Queen asked me if I knew her and if what she had written was true. My surprise was so great that I could not repress a start, which I followed by an exclamation of denial, which appeared to amuse her greatly. "I did not doubt it," she said, "but I'm not sorry to be sure."

Queen Alexandra was accompanied by Lady Gray, her great friend, and the hereditary princess of Greece. After M. Hollman and I had played a duet, she expressed a desire to hear me play alone. As I attempted to lift the lid of the piano, she stepped forward to help me raise it before the maids of honor could intervene. After this slight concert she delivered to each of us, in her own name and in that of the absent king, a gold medal commemorative of artistic merit, and she offered us a cup of tea which she poured with her royal and imperial hands.

Other queens have also received me—Queen Christine of Spain and Queen Amelie of Portugal. After Queen Christine had heard me play on the piano, she expressed a desire to hear me play the organ, and they chose for this an excellent instrument made by Cavaillé-Coll in a church whose name I have forgotten. The day was fixed for this ceremony, which would naturally have been of a private character, when some great ladies lectured the indiscreet queen for daring to resort to a sacred place for any purpose besides taking part in divine services. The queen was displeased by this remonstrance and she responded by coming to the church not only not incognito, but in great state, with the king (he was very young), the ministers and the court, while horsemen stationed at intervals blew their trumpets. I had written a religious march especially for this event, and the Queen kindly accepted its dedication to her. I was a little flustered when she asked me to play the too familiar melody from *Samson et Dalila* which begins *Mon coeur s'ouvre à ta voix*. I had to improvise a transposition suited for the organ, something I had never dreamt of doing. During the performance the Queen leaned her elbow on the keyboard of the organ, her chin resting on one hand and her eyes upturned. She seemed rapt in exstasy which, as may be imagined, was not precisely displeasing to the author.

The press of the day printed delightful articles about the scene, but with no pretense to accuracy. I had nothing to do with that in any way.

Her Majesty Queen Amelie of Portugal once honored me in a distinctive manner. She received me alone without any of her ladies of honor, which allowed her to dispense with all etiquette and to have me sit in a chair near her. In this intimate way she entertained me for three-quarters of an hour asking questions on all sorts of subjects. I had the chance to tell her how the oriental theme of the ballet in *Samson* had been given to me years before by General Yusuf, and to give her many details of that interesting personage of whom she had heard her uncles speak.

"I am going to leave you," she said at last, "but not because I want to. If one conscientiously practices the *metier* of being a queen, one doesn't always find it amusing."

What would that unhappy woman have said, could she have foreseen the calamities that were to befall her!

In Rome I had the honor to be invited to a musicale at Queen Margharita's. The great drawing-rooms were filled with great ladies laden down with family jewels of fabulous value. All the music was terribly serious. Now this kind of music does not make for personal acquaintance, especially as all these great people were victims of a boredom they did their best to conceal. Afterwards the two queens wanted to talk to me. Queen Hélène, who is a violinist, told me that her children were learning the violin and the cello, an arrangement I praised highly, for the exclusive devotion to the piano in these later days has been the death of chamber music and almost of music itself.

In my gallery of sovereigns I cannot forget the gracious Queen of Belgium. I have always seen her, however, in company with her august husband, and this story would become interminable if I were to include "Their Majesties" of the sterner sex — the Emperor of Germany, the Kings of Sweden, Denmark, Spain, Portugal....

As I have had more to do with princes than with sovereigns, my tongue sometimes slips in talking to the latter. As I excused myself one day for addressing the Queen of Belgium as "Highness," she replied, with a smile, "Don't apologize; that recalls good times."

She told me of the time when she and the king, then only heirs apparent, used to go up and down the Mediterranean coast in a little two-seated car. It was during this period that I had the honor of meeting them at the palace of his Serene Highness the Prince of

Monaco, and of having charming and interesting personal conversation with them, for the king is a savant and the queen an artist.

Chapter XXIII

Musical Painters

Ingres was famous for his violin. A single wall separated the apartment where I lived during my childhood and youth from the one where the painter Granger, one of Ingres's pupils, with his wife and daughter, lived. Granger painted the *Adoration of the Wise Men* in the church of Notre Dame de Lorette. I have played with the gilt paper crown which his model wore when posing as one of the three kings. My mother and Mlle. Granger (who later became Madame Paul Meurice) both loved painting and became great friends. They copied together Paul Delaroche's *Enfants d'Edouard* at the Louvre, a picture which was the rage at that time. My mother's paintings, in an admirable state of preservation, may be seen at the museum at Dieppe.

I was introduced to Ingres when I was five years old through the Granger family. The distance from the Rue du Jardinet, where we lived, to the Quai Voltaire was not far, and we often went like a procession—the Grangers, my great-aunt Masson, my mother and I—to call upon Ingres and his wife, a delightfully simple woman whom everyone loved.

Ingres often talked to me about Mozart, Gluck, and all the other great masters of music. When I was six years old, I composed an Adagio which I dedicated to him in all seriousness. Fortunately this masterpiece has been lost. As I already played, and rather nicely for my years, some of Mozart's sonatas, Ingres, in return for my dedication, presented me with a small medallion with the portrait of the author of Don Juan on one side, and this inscription on the other: "To M. Saint-Saëns, the charming interpreter of the divine artist."

He carelessly omitted to add the date of this dedication, which would have increased its interest, for the idea of calling a knee-high youngster of six "M. Saint-Saëns" was certainly unusual.

Ingres, the painter famous for his violin

In addition to the calls I paid him, when I was older I often met the great painter at the house of Frederic Reiset, one of his most ardent admirers. They made much of music in that household and we often heard there Delsarte, the singer without a voice, whom Ingres admired very much. Delsarte and Henri Reber were, in fact, his musical mentors, and, in spite of his pretence of being a great connoisseur, he was in reality their echo. He affected, for example, the most profound contempt for all modern music, and would not even listen to it. In this respect he reflected Reber. Reber used to say quietly in his far-away nasal voice, "You've got to imitate somebody, so the best thing to do is to imitate the ancients, for they are the best." However, he undertook to prove the contrary by writing some particularly individual music, when he thought he was imitating Haydn and Mozart. Some of his works, in their perfection of line, their regard for details, their purity and their moderation remind one of Ingres's drawings which express so much in such a simple way. And Ingres, as well, although he tried to imitate Raphael, could only be himself. Reber would have been worthy of comparison with the painter, if he had had the power and productiveness which distinguish genius.

What about Ingres's violin? Well, I saw this famous violin for the first time in the Montaubon Museum. Ingres never even spoke to me about it. He is said to have played it in his youth, but I could never persuade him to play even the slightest sonata with me. "I used to play," he replied to my entreaties, "the second violin in a quartet, but that is all."

So I think I must be dreaming when I read, from time to time, that Ingres was more appreciative of compliments about his violin-playing than those about his painting. That is merely a legend, but it is impossible to destroy a legend. As the good La Fontaine said:

> "Man is like ice toward truth;
>
> He is like fire to untruth."

I do not know whether Ingres showed talent for the violin in his youth or not. But I can state positively that in his maturity he showed none.

Gustave Doré was also said to be famous on the violin, and his claims to consideration were far from inconsiderable. He had acquired a valuable instrument, on which he used to play Berlioz's *Concertos* with a really extraordinary facility and spirit. These superficial works were enough for his musical powers. The surprising things about his execution was that he never worked at it. If he could not get a thing at once, he gave it up for good and all.

He was a frequent attendant at Rossini's salon, and he belonged to the faction which supported melody and opposed "learned scientific music." His temperament and mine hardly seem compatible, but friendship, like love, has its inexplicable mysteries, and gradually we became the best of friends. We lived in the same quarter and we visited each other frequently. As we almost never were of the same opinion about anything, we had interminable arguments, entirely free from rancor, which we thoroughly enjoyed.

I finally became the confidant of his secret sorrows, and his innermost griefs. He was endowed with a wonderful visual memory, but he made the mistake of never using models, for in his opinion they were useless for an artist who knew his *metier*. So he condemned himself to a perpetual approximation, which was enough for illustrations demanding only life and character, but fatal for large canvasses, with half or full sized figures. This was the cause of his disappointments and failures which he attributed to malevolence and a hostility, which really did exist, but which took advantage of this opportunity to make the painter pay for the exaggerated success of the designer that had been extravagantly praised by the press from the beginning. He laid himself open to criticism through his abuse of his own facility. I have seen him painting away on thirty canvasses at the same time in his immense studio. Three seriously studied pictures would have been worth more.

At heart this great overgrown jovial boy was melancholy and sensitive. He died young from heart disease, which was aggravated by grief over the death of his mother from whom he had never been separated.

I dedicated a slight piece written for the violin to Doré. This was not lost as the one to Ingres was, but it would be entirely unknown had not Johannes Wolf, the violinist of queens and empresses, done me the favor of placing it in his repertoire and bringing his fine talent to its aid.

Hébert was the most serious of the painter-violinists. Down to the end of his life he delighted in playing the sonatas of Mozart and Beethoven, and, from all accounts, he played them remarkably. I can say this only from hearsay, for I never heard him. The few times that I ever saw him at home in my youth, I found him with his brush in hand. I saw him after that only at the Académie, where we sat near each other, and he always greeted me cordially. We talked music from time to time, and he conversed like a connoisseur.

Henri Regnault was the most musical of all the painters whom I have known. He did not need a violin—he was his own. Nature had endowed him with an exquisite tenor voice. It was alluring in its timbre and irresistible in its attractiveness, just as he was himself. He was no "near musician." He loved music passionately, and he was unwilling to sing as an amateur. He took lessons from Romain Bussine at the Conservatoire. He sang to perfection the difficult arias of Mozart's *Don Juan*. He also liked to declaim the magnificent recitative of Pilgrimage in the third act of *Tannhauser*.

As we were friendly and liked the same things, the sympathy which brought us together was quite natural. At the beginning of the war in 1870 I wrote *Les Melodies Persanes* and Regnault was their first interpreter. *Sabre en main* is dedicated to him. But his great success was *Le Cimitière*. Who would have thought as he sang:

> "To-day the roses,
>
> To-morrow the cypress!"

that the prophecy would be realized so soon?

Some imbeciles have written that the loss of Regnault was not to be regretted; that he had said all he had to say. In reality he had given only the prologue of the great poem which he was working out in his brain. He had already ordered canvasses for great compositions which, without a doubt, would have been among the glories of French art.

I saw him for the last time during the siege. He was just starting for drill with his rifle in his hand. One of the four watercolors which were his last work, stood uncompleted on his easel. There was a shapeless spot at the bottom. He held a handkerchief in his free hand. He moistened this from time to time with saliva and kept tapping away on the spot on the picture. To my great astonishment, almost to my fright, I saw roughed out and finished the head of a lion.

A few days afterwards came Buzenval!

When the question of publishing Henri Regnault's letters came up, some phrases referring to me and ranking me above my rivals were found in them. The editor of the letter got into communication with me, read me the phrases, and announced that they were to be suppressed, because they might displease the other musicians.

I knew who the other musicians were, and whose puppet the editor was. It would have been possible, it seems to me, without hurting anyone, to include the exaggerated praise, which, coming from a painter, had no weight, and which would have proved nothing except the great friendship which inspired it. I have always regretted that the public did not learn of the sentiments with which the great artist, whom I loved so much, honored me.

The End